WILKIE

DAVID WILKIE

with
PAT BESFORD
TOMMY LONG

KEMPS, BATH STREET, LONDON E.C.1.

© Pat Besford and Tommy Long 1976
First Published in Great Britain 1976

ISBN 0 905 255 224

Kemps Group (Printers and Publishers) Ltd
1-5 Bath Street
London EC1V 9QA

Printed in Great Britain by
The Halesworth Press Ltd
Halesworth, Suffolk

CONTENTS

LIST OF ILLUSTRATIONS

(In Order of Appearance)

Picture credits

All pictures from Tony Duffy, All-Sport Photos Ltd
with the exception of those from

The Wilkie family (pages 1, 2, 3, 32); Frank Thomas (6, 7);
Daily Express (16); Bill Black (16); Derek Rowe (17); Daily Mirror
(26, 31); Sports Aid Foundation (28); London Weekend TV (29)
and Platignum Guild (30)

"I've had my moment, now it's sharing time."

David Wilkie

This book is dedicated to all those who had a part in David Wilkie's success.

London
October, 1976

Pat Besford
Tommy Long

PRESENTING DAVID WILKIE M.B.E.

A portrait of a champion

The green-blue water gleamed and sparkled. The white and red lane-lines that divided the fifty metre pool into neat identical parts were stretched tight. The banks of orange and yellow seats, rising on each side of the arena, were packed to over-flowing. And the massed lights blazed down from the spirals snaking across and around the huge, high, domed roof.

A smiling, dark-haired young man, with a moustache and side-burns, raised his right hand in salute. On his left chest were the five ring Olympic symbol, the Union Jack and the place and the year. Around his neck, proudly worn, hung a gold medal. And as the crowds cheered and stamped, waved flags and whistled, screamed and clapped, and the music blared, Olympic swimming champion and world record-breaker David Wilkie of Great Britain acknowledged the acclaim he deserved on July 24th, 1976, his golden day. It proved to be Britain's only individual gold medal in Montreal.

Now the crowds, the cameras and the world's greatest swimmers have left the Piscine Olympique, perhaps never to come back in such force or quality again. The great grey electronic results board, whose lights had flashed to signal world record after world record — and none finer than Wilkie's one — may be out of date before such exalted company return. And after the gladiators have gone, even the finest Olympic stadium becomes a shell, peopled by ghosts, echoing with whispers of what has been, of what will never be again.

Wilkie's victory in the 200 metres breaststroke was shattering in execution, overwhelming, magnificent for everyone who saw it. For David, the moment that was his alone, the moment when he received his golden medal tribute, was the perfect climax to his sporting career. It was done. He had done it and it was wonderful.

Now the cheers have subsided. Now, in the history books of swimming, David Wilkie's name is recorded along with all the other winners of Olympic titles since 1896. Now, in the quiet of a deed well done, it is possible to look back on the life and times of a reluctant champion, who reached the top almost in spite of himself.

The story of Wilkie's progress up the steep swimming ladder to the very pinnacle tells how the dawdling footsteps of the unwilling schoolboy were turned into the determined tread of the mature adult, who set about his Olympic task with single-minded concentration.

His childhood, the carefree life with his family in Ceylon . . . the shock of his sudden exile to a Scottish boarding school . . . the influences of the many people who recognised his ability and potential . . . and the final comprehension of a unique champion, who learned the hard way and succeeded in the end have made writing this book a task of fascinating discovery.

It is said that getting words out of Wilkie is like squeezing water out of a dry towel. That is not always true, yet David is a very private person. So memories, impressions, fleeting moments have been collected and culled from many places and many people to present the how it was and how it is.

David responds to crowds in public, but does not like to be crowded in private. He can be gracious and charming and gently witty in company, yet he is completely his own man, a loner who enjoys being by himself, who can and does disappear for hours to do his own thing.

There is no question about his ability, or his quality as a competitor of high courage, who cannot be intimidated. He has learned the tricks and the tactics and can put them into practice coolly and calmly. Yet he is a complex character too, capable of making the most horrific mistakes, two of which resulted in his not even reaching the finals of events he could and should have won.

His 200 metres world record of 2 min. 15.11 sec. in Montreal is considered by swimming experts from many countries outside Britain to be the greatest of all the records set in the Olympic swimming pool. As the Australian "International Swimmer" reported: "One must ask what sort of swimmer, what kind of man, can break a 200 metres world record by 3.10 seconds? Just fantastic." Yet, at home, it is probable that few realise the full significance of what David did — and he certainly won't mention it.

He is inordinately proud of what he has achieved and that he was able to do it for Britain. But it took his girl friend Kate three weeks to discover that he was a World champion when she first met him in 1973.

Swimming has given Wilkie the chance to circle the world. He has competed on all five Continents. He has been to most countries of Europe, from Iceland to Italy, the Soviet Union to Spain . . . to Asia . . . Africa . . . east to west across Canada . . . the United States . . . the West Indies . . . Colombia and Puerto Rico . . . and to far-away New Zealand.

He has won fifteen major swimming medals, eight gold, four silver and three bronze. Three were Olympic, a silver from Munich 1972 and a gold and a silver from Montreal. He earned five at the World championships in Belgrade in 1973 and Cali, Colombia, two years later — three gold and two bronze. His European haul from Vienna in 1974 was two golds and a silver and he also took two golds, a silver and a bronze from the Commonwealth Games of 1970 and 1974 in Edinburgh and Christchurch, New Zealand.

His thirty major records split up as three World, nine European and 18 Commonwealth. He was never beaten over 200 metres breaststroke from September 1973 and he retired, undefeated, in the summer of 1976 holding every honour open to him for this event, as Olympic, World, European and Commonwealth champion and record-holder. No swimmer has ever been able to do this before and few are likely to repeat it.

Wilkie was Europe's swimming "Man of the Year" for 1974 and 1975 and, not surprisingly, has been named again for 1976. He has headed six annual world best performance lists for his speciality breaststroke and medley events. He has . . . well, the list is endless.

At home, he was elected "Sportsman of the Year" by the Sports Writers' Association of Great Britain in 1975 and by Scotland as their "Sportsman of the Year" in 1972 and "Swimmer of the Year" in 1970, 1972, 1973, 1974 and 1975. It will be the surprise of the year if David does not receive at least the last two awards again in 1976.

Condensing seven years of achievement into a few paragraphs is absolutely misleading. Statistics cannot express or explain all that had to be done by a remarkable young man to make these achievements possible. David is not a swimming machine, programmed to perform at the blast of a starting gun. He is a very human being.

1954-1965

CEYLON

The carefree days

WILKIE — on March 8 in Colombo
Ceylon, to Jean (nee McDonald)
and Harry Wilkie, a son David
Andrew, a brother for Caroline.

A small notice for a small arrival in an Aberdeen paper back in 1954 may not have meant much to anyone outside the Wilkie family and friends and there was no background to suggest that baby David Andrew might one day bring credit to Britain at the highest level of amateur sporting competition in the world.

Only his birth sign, Pisces "The Fish", gave a possible clue to a starry future in the water, though there must have been millions born under this sign who never even learned to swim. Still, there isn't any doubt that young David Wilkie liked the water, he liked the beach, the sea and the fish that swam in the warm Indian Ocean around Ceylon where the family lived . . . his father Harry, a management executive, mother Jean, a former secretary, and one-year-older Caroline.

In those days Colombo was all very colonial, a splendid city for the expatriots of many countries whose family entertainment centered around the club — in this case the Colombo Swimming Club, which was THE place for diplomats, the United Nations staff, the business and professional people, their wives and children.

David has vivid memories of those first 11 years of his life in Ceylon and although he has not been back, except for holidays, since 1965, he would like to return there again one day — if only for a visit. He can still see in his mind's eye the Wilkie home in Colombo . . . the big old colonial club building, with its swimming, boating and paddling pools . . . beach holidays . . . and fishing with his father.

Life was good then for the Wilkie children. There were servants at home, a cook, houseboy and a nanny to clear up after them and take care of them if parents were not around — and at that time Harry and Jean Wilkie, so far away from their native Aberdeen, had a pleasant and active social life.

David remembers Christmases in Ceylon, with the tree planted in a special red bucket that was kept in the garage until the next year, the excitement of presents and the wondering why was Father Xmas's handwriting the same as Mum's and Dad's! Most of all, though he thinks his parents were strict with him and his sister — not particularly so in his mother's opinion — it is the togetherness of the family that David recalls and talks of with genuinely fond affection.

"Our closeness was the important thing of my childhood. We did everything together . . . looking back I think my schooldays in Ceylon were more enjoyable than anywhere. It was a good time in my life and we had a lot of fun.

"After school we used to go to the club and our parents would meet us there for tea or dinner. We didn't have to pay for anything at the swimming club . . . just sign a chit with our parents' number on it. So we were always very free with milk-shakes, Coca-Colas, ice-creams and things like that. The only time we worried was just before they got their monthly bill! We used to be told we were spending too much, but by the next month it would be the same thing all over again.

"The ocean was just over the wall from the pool, so it was a nice location. We children weren't supposed to go over the wall because there was a railway line there and I suppose parents were afraid their children would get run over. But we used to sneak over and swim in the ocean.

"We, that is the whole family, spent all our holidays together at different places in Ceylon. The favourite was Hikkadawu, a really beautiful place where we used to go for a couple of weeks at a time and we had rooms right on the beach, only about 50 feet from the water.

"I suppose it was there my interest started in marine biology.

Hikkadawu had a reef only about 15 feet off shore — at low tide it was completely uncovered — and my father and sister and I used to go exploring on it. Fishing, too, though we never seemed to catch much . . . I think my Dad caught two fish, once, but I never caught anything.

"One night I remember I got some shrimps from the kitchen for bait, made up a fishing tackle, stuck the shrimps on the hooks, tied on a rock for a weight and threw the baited hooks into the sea. I expected to come back in the morning and find I'd caught three or four fish.

"I couldn't sleep very well that night . . . too excited at the thought of reeling in all my fish, but when I did go down next day everything had disappeared — hooks, line and sinker. I don't know what happened, but it was a big disappointment.

"At that time I was interested in insects, too, putting different species together to see what would happen. I got stung many times and vowed I wouldn't touch them again. Until next day . . .! We used to collect hornets nests in jam jars and doing that once I got very badly bitten in the corner of an eye.

"Once I dared a friend to stand in a nest of red ants for five minutes and I promised him a milk-shake (to be paid for by Mum and Dad — of course) if he did it. But the ants bit him so much all over his legs he jumped out after two minutes. What about the milk-shake? No, I didn't get it for him . . . he wasn't there long enough."

Swimming came about as naturally almost as eating, sleeping and getting into mischief, so much so that David really doesn't remember exactly when he learned.

"I swam practically before I walked . . . I was in the water at three months old and I could swim a length of the 100-foot club pool when I was about three — at least so I've been told. I suppose I learned by looking at other people, picking up what they did, though my father helped me along. Everyone swam in Ceylon."

By the time he was eight years old, he and sister Caroline had made three trips to their parents' Scottish "hame" in the north of the British Isles when Harry and Jean Wilkie went on three-yearly leave. Britain made little impression on two-year-old David, but he vaguely remembers attending Broomhill School in Aberdeen at five and definitely remembers the six months he spent there at eight. It

The future Olympic champion in the toddlers' pool at the Colombo Swimming Club in 1955, having a go at butterfly.

Nanny helps baby David while sister Caroline concentrates on her beach bucket (1955) and, five years later, Caroline, friend Lesley (centre) and a dark-haired David. (Courtesy Wilkie family.)

Christmas in Colombo 1954, when David was nine months old. (Below): With Mum, Dad and Caroline . . . and already showing signs of the big feet and supple ankles which did so much for his swimming 20 years on.

Scotland's Dave the Brave (right) in his first kilt (1957) — the McDonald clan tartan of his mother's family, which the Wilkies also are entitled to wear.

was then that the realisation grew on him that Ceylon and Scotland were different countries, seeing snow at Christmas for the first time and even feeling slightly regretful at leaving new friends to go back East at the end of his father's leave.

But the climate of life on that island in the sun was turning cold for David Andrew. And when the shattering blow came in 1965, when education — where else but in Scotland — took precedence over life as a family, David could not believe it.

"I don't think we ever considered that one day we would be sent off to boarding school. Even when we went to Scotland that year we never thought we wouldn't be going back to Colombo as usual . . . for a whole year in fact.

"We didn't understand and we couldn't accept it. I couldn't anyway . . . I just wanted to get out of that place. Looking back, I suppose my first two years at boarding school were sheer hell."

3

1965-1970

WARRENDER

A War without end

Scots have a pet name for their capital city. They call it "Auld Reekie". But back in the autumn of 1965, if the then lonely 11-year-old David Wilkie could have pressed a magic button, the city of Edinburgh, the Daniel Stewarts College where he was a boarding pupil and the Warrender Baths Swimming Club of which he was an unwilling member would have all dropped into the Firth of Forth. And, as they disappeared, a small sun-bronzed forced exile from Ceylon would have danced in high delight.

As David said: "Life was sheer hell." If he had to be thrust away by himself, away from his loved family and good friends in Colombo, from all the sunny scenes of his childhood, then by himself was where he was going to be . . . by himself he was going to decide what he did and when he did and if he did. And if that meant war to the end with Warrender, then war it was.

He was very polite about it. He did not make it too obvious. He just opted out and it took a long, long time and much behind the scenes loving and caring by the club members and the staff at the school to coax David out of his studied shell of indifference to everything and everyone, to bring him out of his lonely little world.

Harry and Jean Wilkie knew that David was unhappy, but they were in a cleft stick. They had to stay in Ceylon. That was where Harry's job was. And David had to be educated which was not possible in Colombo. They could only hope that things would work out.

David came to Warrender through an introduction from the Drumsheugh baths, the nearest pool to his new school. And it is probable Harry did this because he knew of his son's love for swimming. But the good idea almost worked in reverse.

Frank Thomas, at that time chief coach and mainstay of the club's competitive programme, remembers the day he first met Master Wilkie, age 11.

"He was brought along by his parents, friendly and charming people. He was a wee lad, in his Daniel Stewarts school uniform — short shorts and all — and a fringe. Even then his silence was most marked."

David recalls his long-ago memories like this:

"I suppose the day I joined Warrender was when my swimming career started and almost abruptly finished. After two weeks of it I was ready to quit and when my parents went back to Ceylon that is what David Wilkie proceeded to do. I never went training, I believe I skipped it for a whole year without anybody finding out.

"Frank Thomas chucked me out of the club and at that time this wasn't any hardship on my part. The boarding housemaster and my Dad weren't too pleased about that, so I was reinstated and made a go of it the second time, but still without much enthusiasm.

"One of the troubles was that I did not make any effort to get friendly with the Warrender crowd. My life was surrounded by the people at school — not the day boys, but those in the boarding house who were in a similar situation to me, having to be away from home.

"I could understand them, but I couldn't understand Warrender and I suppose they couldn't really understand me either. I never tried to make friends with them and maybe they didn't try to make friends with me." In this, David was wrong . . . as shall be explained later.

"I suppose I kept swimming from 12-15 with various mischievous acts to break the monotony . . . skipping training with nobody finding out . . . coming back to school having been out and wetting my hair so they would think I had been training when I actually hadn't. Instead I'd been skiving around town, wasting time, doing nothing.

"I can remember walking along the street to Warrender baths on Sunday afternoons hoping and praying that the pool would be shut for some reason, but it never was. And if nobody spotted me as I walked along then I would say to myself 'Do you really

want to go training?' and the answer, usually, was 'No'. So I
would walk back down the road and go for a coffee or something
. . . waiting for the hour to pass so that I could go back to
school.

"Maybe it was my fault. I was disheartened at having to go
and didn't want to have anything to do with those who were
trying to make me train. I did try to get some of my school
friends to come swimming and get interested and one boy, Ian
McKechnie, did, once, but he didn't go back again.

"The boarders stuck together in everything, even against the
day boys, even as teams with the boarders against the others. I
was not very interested in work but liked games, soccer particularly and other extra-curricular activities. The school sports,
rugby and cricket, weren't very interesting to me — I never really
enjoyed physical sports and rugby was always so damn cold that
I couldn't hold on to the ball. I always played as a left wing in
rugby because I could run quite fast. I didn't mind that position,
because I didn't have to get into the scrum."

The Thomas family memories of young **Wilkie** run along similar
lines though, of course, from the other side of the canvas. Frank's
mother will never forget the time David came to stay for a week and
the haunting loneliness, reserve and extreme silence of the boy.

Frank says:

"My mother was affected quite incredibly by the way David
moved so softly about the house. If she wanted him, she had to go
and search for him. Sometimes, he would vanish completely,
without a word of farewell and return equally silently and go
straight to his room. One day she found him playing a tape
recorder, sitting on the floor with the music turned down so low he
had to have his head right down to hear . . . most unusual for a
youngster.

"There was little communication with David then, and even
at the end of his seven years in Edinburgh things were hardly
changed, except that he was showing considerable application at
swimming — once he had got into the water.

"We were quickly aware that we had a problem on our hands
and elaborate efforts and arrangements were made to try to draw
David out. But I cannot say it was a great success . . . he somehow
eluded all the overtures.

"We looked around for outgoing types to jolly him along. If we went away as a team we hand-picked members to travel with him, to try and get him to talk. After one four-hour journey, I heard he had spoken only 12 words.

"One regular club place was the Aviemore Sports Centre in the Cairngorm, where we went for week-end training. Even there David tended to keep himself to himself. I nipped this in the bud a bit, by telling all the squad they must at least go around in pairs so that no one was left alone . . . and this was said with only David in mind.

"While it was difficult on these trips to persuade him to become part of the group, there was never any question of David breaking rules or getting out of line. If I asked him to be in a place by a certain time he would be there. One of the many who did a lot for David at that time was David Kidd, then President of the club. He took young David to a cinema in Aviemore and said "Wait there till I come for you'. And wait there he did.

"And that was the paradox of David. Once he actually got to the pool his work was absolutely terrific, one couldn't ask for more. He trained hard, he led the others, he always listened to what was being said. And once he had absorbed an instruction, it never had to be said again and within days it had become part of his stroke. Once there he became one of those special kind of swimmers that every coach dreams of having on his squad, an example to everyone. THE TROUBLE WAS TO GET HIM THERE."

And getting Wilkie to water occupied many hours for Frank Thomas, a quantity surveyor by profession.

"Because the morning training started so early, David was supposed to make his own arrangements for getting up and to the pool. As a result, we rarely saw him. Later, from about 1968 on, I used to drive from the south side to the north side of the city to pick him up. I felt it was important to get him training and I used to sit outside the boarding house waiting for him to appear. Almost half the time, and certainly once in three, he just never did appear and there was no way I could get in to find him.

"One of his excuses for not turning up was that he had over-slept (and he could sleep until midday, given a chance) so I bought him an alarm clock. Yet he was still erratic with his time-keeping.

He had either 'forgotten' to set the alarm, or set it for 'the wrong time', etc., etc. After a couple of weeks he said the clock was broken, so I got it mended, but he didn't get any better.

"During his second year at Warrender he was kicked out of the squad, reluctantly, because of his bad attendance. David's reasons for not coming were countless; he'd missed the bus . . . overslept . . . gone to a football match . . . visited his aunt in Edinburgh . . . anything at all that enabled him to skip swimming. Yes, he always had reasons, but never made excuses . . . he just didn't appear. And he would have been kicked out many more times if there hadn't been a unique something about him which made me say 'Give it another try'.

"So, instead of chucking him out again, I had many telephone conversations with his housemasters to see what could be done — and this went on year, after year, after year. His then housemaster was Douglas McMahon, a top-class rugby referee, who was tremendously helpful. Few schools, I believe, could or would have gone to so much trouble over David as Daniel Stewarts did. Later, Alan Fox became housemaster and the same kind of discussions were repeated and with the headmaster Mr. Bellis.

"Even after his Commonwealth Games bronze medal success in 1970 David was still up to his old tricks and definitely hadn't got the message that he had great potential . . . that the swimming world was his oyster. He missed early morning training, turned up late in the evening, or didn't come at all. He would disappear . . . say, up to his uncle in Aberdeen, without a word. So the Wilkie saga continued.

"Then the boarding house itself began to check more on David's movements in an effort to pin him down, to make sure when he left to go swimming he really did go. And in October 1971 the school pounced. He was gated for two weeks and had to miss representing Scotland against England and Wales in the Bologna Trophy contest at Grimsby.

"What David had been doing was to leave school with his towel and trunks, ostensibly for training but never getting there. The official school statement said: 'Special arrangements were made both at Daniel Stewarts College and the Boarding House so that David Wilkie could train for and compete in International events. This arrangement naturally assumed his cooperation. The reason why he now cannot take part in any contest until mid-term concerns only Wilkie and his school, but these have been fully explained to the National Swimming Authority and have been accepted as entirely reasonable.' "

David actually got caught out because Frank Thomas telephoned housemaster Fox to ask where his missing swimmer was, to be told that he had gone swimming! And the truth came out. Says David:

"I was upset at that because I did want to swim in the Bologna. It was boring being stuck at school at the week-end and not being allowed to go out . . . I'D RATHER HAVE GONE SWIMMING THAN THAT!"

Inevitably, Scottish swimming abounds with Wilkie stories. Bill Law, the Scottish diving coach and a former Warrender president, recalls a continental tour in 1969 when the team travelled 2,000 miles by bus around Western Europe. And David read comics almost all the way.

He was occupied in a similar fashion, sitting on a chair behind the starting block, as he waited for the start of his first big-time final, the 200 metres at the 1970 Commonwealth Games, despite the fact that he was Scotland's only swimming medal hope. Cool . . . cool!

Gordon Stirton, David's great Warrender rival and friend, has his own collection of Wilkie-isms. In the days when Frank went to pick up David at school, the other members of the squad used to tell Wilkie to be late in the morning. For that would mean coach Thomas being late as well — and they would only have to do half a normal work-out. "This is news to me" said Frank years later.

There was the time, after the Commonwealth Games, when 16-year-old David was about to go home to Colombo for a holiday and he filled a suitcase completely with packets of Sugar Frosties, because he couldn't get these in Ceylon.

. . . and the time Gordon and David shared a room in Norway, the only one with a balcony, with a flag pole outside. They "borrowed" the girls' nighties, then hung them on the flag pole . . . and it rained.

. . . and, during an Eight-Nations contest in Switzerland, some of the boys went to a disco and ordered a round of drinks, then discovered it would cost £20. So they left the drinks on the table, quietly but hurriedly climbed out through the men's loo window and disappeared into the night.

This was the light side of David, but he was still incredibly shy and introverted . . . very much a loner. Frank Thomas has a point when he says:

> "If it hadn't been for Warrender, David would not have continued swimming past the 1960's. This is one of the fantastic things about the club . . . swimmers aren't just treated as swimmers, but also as human beings and I believe the warmth and help he received when he was with us must have helped him through the most difficult growing-up stage of his life, even if he wasn't aware of it at the time."

The troubles were forgotten in 1972. David Wilkie was made a Life Member of the Warrender Baths Swimming Club, following his silver medal success at the Munich Olympic Games.

4

1970-1971

EDINBURGH & BARCELONA

The one who did least did the best

Just as the ugly little duckling of the Danny Kaye song turned out to be a very white swan indeed, so it was in swimming for David Wilkie. He opened his juvenile competitive wings on butterfly in Ceylon, even won his first medal on this style there, switched to free-style when he went to Edinburgh and also dabbled a little with backstroke and breaststroke.

But the true potential on the breaststroke that was to make him a world star did not show until 1969 and then it came about almost by accident. David was a member of a Warrender club squad who toured West Germany in the spring of that year and, as always happens on these kind of trips, had to tackle a variety of different events. One was the 100 metres breaststroke and, out of the blue, he gave Scottish champion Gordon Stirton one hell of a fright by coming close to beating him. That performance clicked with David and also triggered off the decision by coach Frank Thomas to develop Wilkie's talent for this specialised stroke.

The race with Stirton and the fact that Gordon was around in competition and training was just the thing that was needed to rouse "Jungle Boy" Wilkie — as his Warrender team-mates called him because of his tanned skin and Ceylon origins. Stirton was never a great stylist, but he was an aggressive performer and, in David's mind, became the man to beat.

"Gordon was always better than me and I looked up to him as a person I would never be able to beat. So when I finally dead-heated with him in the East District trials — in my best time by three seconds — I was really excited. I still didn't realise then that I could be a good swimmer, so Gordon was an important stepping-stone in my swimming career . . . probably my first stepping-stone.

"The training I did in those days wasn't very much. I was satis-fied with myself if I averaged 20,000 yards *a week*. I thought that was enough, because I wasn't involved as a serious swimmer and I wasn't interested in doing well. And even as I improved, had more success and was beating Gordon consistently, my attitude still didn't change. I was still uncommitted."

So there was David at the end of 1969 with a best time of 2 min. 57.9 for 200 metres to his credit. And there was Frank Thomas with the problem of motivating Wilkie, whom he now believed had a great breaststroke potential, for the Commonwealth Games the following summer.

Whatever was said, it had an immediate effect and David's times began to show it. He set three Scottish junior records in January and February 1970 and a senior one of 2 min. 42.7 sec. for 220 yards during his first British international trials appearance at Crystal Palace in March.

Two weeks later, at Paisley, he won the Scottish short-course 200 yards title in 2:20.5 and was second in the 100 yards. His first Scottish cap came the next week, against Norway at Larvik, where he won the 200 metres (short-course) in 2:36.3 — and in those three races, Gordon Stirton finished behind Wilkie each time.

British representative honours came to David for the first time in April when he was chosen to swim against the Soviet Union in the opening gala at the new Royal Commonwealth Pool in Edinburgh. Unfortunately his debut did not quite match the occasion, for he finished only third in the 200 metres, twelve seconds behind Russia's Eugeniy Mikhailov. However, on the credit side, Wilkie's 2:39.7, another Scottish long-course record, represented a personal im-provement of twelve seconds in eight weeks and almost double that since the beginning of the year.

Scotland's elaborate preparations for their very own Common-wealth Games in Edinburgh, from July 16th to 25th, also included matches against Iceland in Reykjavik in June, when David came second in the 100 and 200 metres, and Denmark in Edinburgh in July. In the Danish match Wilkie claimed his first British record in winning the 200 metres in 2:32.9 and he also took the 100 metres in Scottish figures of 1:10.8.

Sadly for the host nation, the big build-up programme brought the swimming squad to their peak just a few days too soon — and by the time the Games opened many were "over the top". But not Wilkie.

With the second fastest 200 metres time in the Commonwealth, he was Scotland's only medal hope . . . and the hope was realised. Wilkie cut his British record to 2:32.5 in a heat and won the bronze with a 2:32.9 in the final, finishing behind gold medal winner Bill Mahony of Canada and Paul Jarvie of Australia. David was also fifth in the 100 metres breaststroke in 1:11.0, but with only the tenth best time of 2:25.6, failed to qualify for the final of the 200 metres medley.

The reaction was a typical Wilkie understatement: "I swam quite well," but then this almost in-built reluctance to be involved came to the surface again with "but we did have a six-weeks training camp before the Games and I couldn't do anything else but swim, so I suppose I trained very hard. I was the only Scot to win a swimming medal . . . so the person who did the best had really put the least into it!"

In a way, the same could be said about Wilkie's work at Daniel Stewarts College.

"I was never a good student, never worked hard. I did my work, but that was all and I didn't do anything extra. We used to have two hours prep each night, but most of us tried to do it as quickly as possible and sneak comics in with us and hide them behind text books. If the housemasters spotted us, we had to do extra work, but in most cases they didn't.

"So I went through school doing the least amount of work possible, but I passed seven O levels with average grades and two highers, which I suppose wasn't bad. Compared with other people in swimming, it seems I had quite a high level of success."

It might have been expected that winning a medal in the Games might have inspired David to bigger and better things. But NO! Although, on the strength of his performance in Edinburgh, he was chosen as the only breaststroke team member for Britain in the European championships in Barcelona at the end of August, David was determined to return to Colombo for a holiday. And go he did.

"It was important for me to go to Ceylon. I felt I needed a holiday and as I only saw my parents a few times a year there was no way

I was going to attend any training camp before Barcelona, or miss my summer holiday.

"I didn't really want to take part in the European champion-ships — that's how important my holiday was to me and how un-important was the swimming meeting. I cabled my father to ask what I should do and the fact that he told me to come for my holiday, then go to Spain was an indication of how little he or I understood what taking part in an event at that level was all about.

"Frank Thomas set me a programme of training for the three weeks I was in Ceylon, but I didn't stick to it very rigidly. It wasn't much fun going training when your friends are having a good time. I probably only did it for a couple of days a week as a kind of token effort.

"I arrived in Barcelona extremely out of shape, about a week before the start. Even the girls were beating me on breaststroke . . . that's how bad I was. Of course, it was a lack of any involvement on my part and I don't suppose that many people have gone into a meeting of that quality without even training for it."

David wasn't fooling about his condition. He was last in his heat of the 100 metres breaststroke in 1 min. 12.4 sec., nearly 1½ seconds below his Edinburgh effort and only three men out of the 21 entries were slower.

He was seventh out of eight in his heat of the 200 metres breast-stroke, 7½ seconds slower than his Commonwealth Games bronze medal performance and 20th out of 22 competitors.

Britain had to swim David in the medley relay team because there was no one else to take on the breaststroke leg. "That was a mistake. The selectors should never take only one person to cover an event, especially a relay, in case something goes wrong."

And although the squad of Mike Richards, Wilkie, Mike Bailey and Malcolm Windeatt managed to scrape into the final, they finished last, 15 seconds behind the winners East Germany. Wilkie swam his leg nearly three seconds slower than the slowest man and six seconds worse than the fastest.

"Looking back I'm ashamed of myself. But, at the time, I simply did not realise how important the event was, or my responsibilities."

5

1972

MUNICH

The first touch of silver success . . .

The year of the 1972 Munich Games was heralded with the boldest experiment in the history of British swimming and the fact that it came almost to nothing was not the fault of those who conceived it.

Basically, the plan involved setting up a centre for Olympic hopefuls in York, where the swimmers could work, or go to school, yet also train in a squad situation. Then, after the official Olympic trials, the whole team would prepare together, first in Southampton and later in Coventry, before going to Germany.

But the whole structure came tumbling down in near ruin with a drug scandal, newspaper front page headlines, sacked swimmers, charges on television and protests by members of Parliament. It was an unhappy affair, perhaps not handled as sympathetically as it might have been and the eyes of the Press and the British public suddenly became focussed on a group of unthinking young people.

Some swimmers — an unspecified number, for many names were mentioned in whispers and in private — had indulged in a little pot-smoking to while away the time between training. Quiet action, possibly, could have avoided a drama, but the happening became public knowledge when, following telephone calls from a mystery lady to newspapers and other people, the police appeared on the scene. The "dark lady" was never identified, but three of the swimmers were thrown out of the team, one of whom subsequently won a court case to prove his innocence, while others escaped and did not even have their names taken.

The fact that only three British swimmers — Brian Brinkley, Dorothy Harrison and David Wilkie — reached finals in Munich and that Wilkie won a swimming medal, a silver in the 200 metres breaststroke, was nothing to do with the pre-Games training sensations. As David says so bluntly:

"I suppose we were pressurised by the Press over this (the drug business) and the fact could be used as an excuse. But I don't think it was a valid one. I was sad about what happened, but I didn't let myself get upset.

"And the story that Britain did badly in the Games — and we did overall — because of other people's mistakes was wrong. It wasn't the fault of the manager John Verrier, or the coach Hammy Bland, or anyone else. It was the fault of the swimmers themselves.

"Most of those who went to Munich allowed themselves to be overawed by the occasion and by the people they were going to swim against. And to a few, quite a few in fact, it was just another trip. They were there to swim but, most of all, to have a good time. They weren't there to compete against the best in the world and try to beat them or, at least, to do their fastest times. They were there just to get in, swim, get it over with and get on with the good time.

"Yet we were all well conditioned, all in good shape. And although the drug business, which started when we were in Southampton and came to a head in Coventry, was said to have affected a lot of people, I don't think that was really true, because it didn't disrupt our training at all."

That is the mature David of 1976 talking. Back in Edinburgh in 1972 it took a straight-talking show-down with his Warrender club coaches Frank Thomas and John Ashton to get the wayward Wilkie to work. Thomas says:

"Early in the year, when the Olympics were well and truly looming, David was not even committed to trying to get into the British team for Munich. He was as irregular with his training as he ever had been. John and I had many serious chats with him and he promised to improve, but he never did. With so much at stake and so much potential in the boy, it was the worst time I can remember.

"The crunch came when he disappeared for a week without a word. When he came back we took him upstairs at the Queen Margaret College pool, sat him down and laid it on the line for 30 minutes. We told him again about his potential and his ability . . .

that he would have to train hard to go to the Olympics . . . that it would be crazy to quit swimming — *which is what he was thinking of doing."*

The force of their arguments had some effect on David, whose memories of the incident go like this:

"Frank and John said if I wasn't going to stick to swimming properly it wasn't really worth continuing. They laid down a programme for me for a month, with 10 sessions a week, and said if I didn't get through the work then it was all over . . . finished. Frank said he had known me long enough to say this and that was it.

"At the back of my mind there had been a thought that I could be a great swimmer, but I was just too lazy. I really was not interested, certainly not excited. Basically I suppose I simply had no desire to compete. But I did everything Frank wanted me to do and I suppose that was the beginning.

"Then Hammy Bland, who had been coach to the Olympic squad in Mexico City in 1968 and was to do a similar job in Munich, came to Edinburgh to see Frank and ask if he would let me go to the York scheme. And the decision that I should totally commit myself to the Olympic idea was probably one of the most important in my life — even if it did come late, with less than three months to prepare to compete against the greatest swimmers in the world.

"Even then I did not realise I had a chance of making a final, for my best times were about 1 min. 8.8 sec. for 100 metres and 2 min. 30 sec. for 200 metres, and those weren't going to set the pool on fire.

"I arrived in York after my higher examinations, having left school by this time. I wasn't in good shape, but the squad were a great bunch of lads and I really enjoyed working with Hammy. He was a most interesting coach, gave us plenty of variety in our pool work, got everyone training hard against each other and everything went very well indeed. The top British swimmers had never been brought together in this way before and though I don't want to appear to be pushing the York scheme, I do think it provided the springboard into what British swimming needed."

York certainly lifted Wilkie to a new height of endeavour. The discipline and the challenge of training with and against two other very promising young breaststroke hopes — David Leigh from Sheffield and Paul Naisby from Sunderland, who won places in the Munich team and, four years later, also went to Montreal — gave Wilkie a new feeling. In a few weeks, he got through distances he had never done before, not because he could not have done them in Edinburgh, but because he did not want to do them there. Yet a place in an Olympic final wasn't even a pipe dream, it was hardly to be considered.

At the end of July, during an eight-nations contest in the Royal Commonwealth Pool in Edinburgh, Wilkie improved his 200 metres time by more than three seconds to set his first Commonwealth record of 2 min. 26.76 sec. This was just over three seconds outside the world figures of America's Brian Job and, suddenly, the reluctant Wilkie was a potential finalist in Munich for the 200 metres, though as a sprinter he was a long way out of the reckoning.

Wilkie confessed later that Munich got him excited about being able to compete at world level. While most of the rest of the British team allowed themselves to be over-powered and submerged by the sheer size of the Olympic occasion, it acted in absolutely the reverse way for David. He wasn't intimidated, he enjoyed the colour and the drama, the noise and the excitement. For the first time, he was involved, a true competitor and a budding champion.

"The Olympics of 1972 was a very drastic point in my life, when a big change came about . . . when I began to mature . . . when I learned that I was a good competitor and had a lot of confidence in myself.

"I had the 100 metres first and came in eighth, which was really a blow to me to be in such a low position and it set me back a bit for the 200 metres."

The sauce of the lad — at that moment, hardly dry behind the ears in the big-time swimming scene, after years of dragging his feet and not wanting to be involved. Here he was, having the cheek to be disappointed with a place, even if it was the last one, in an Olympic final — something many dream about and very few achieve. Having said that, it was a wonderful attitude for Wilkie to have.

He had won his 100 metres heat on August 29th in 1 min. 6.35 sec., a Commonwealth record and 1.35 sec. faster than the Olympic winning time of Don McKenzie (U.S.A.) in 1968. Wilkie cut his time

Ceylon in the sixties.
David and Caroline in
1961 with the early
Wilkie collection of
swimming trophies and
medals . . . with Nanny
in the garden in 1962
(below) and playing
rickshaw boy with
Mum in 1969.
(Courtesy Wilkie
family.)

THE THREE FACES OF DAVID WILKIE

1970 . . . the unwilling schoolboy on his way to a bronze medal in the 200 metres breast-stroke at the Commonwealth Games in Edinburgh.

1971 . . . competing at the National short-course championships at Worthing. Note the goggles, from then on to be a part of the Wilkie image and (below):

1973 . . . and it is World champion and record-holder Wilkie in Belgrade. Now the Wilkie trade-marks include cap, moustache and side-burns.

David in 1970, at the time of his Commonwealth Games bronze-medal success.

A Warrender club trio of Scottish internationals, circa 1971 [left to right] Gordo Stirton, Alex Devlin and Wilkie. (Photo: courtesy Frank Thomas)

by one tenth of a second in the semi-final that evening, but this only gave him fifth in his race and eighth fastest overall. And in the final, the following night, Wilkie was eighth again (1:6.52) with the gold, silver and bronze medals going to Japan's Nobutaka Taguchi (1:4.94, a world record), Tom Bruce (1:5.43) and John Hencken (1:5.61), both of the United States.

Three days later, Wilkie took his first, firm strokes towards what can only be considered as a shock medal. Again, he was in heat no. 3 of six heats. And, again, he touched first. His 2 min. 24.54 sec. was the second fastest of the 40 competitors, beaten only by Taguchi (2:23.45). It was a Commonwealth record and it was 3.16 seconds better than the 1968 winning time of Mexico's Felipe Munoz. Hencken, soon to assume the mantle of Wilkie's career-long rival, clocked 2:24.88.

Yet it wasn't his record, nor the fact that he had qualified for the final so high up the list, that were uppermost in David's thoughts. He was much more concerned about how his parents could get tickets for the "sold-out" pool to watch him swim in the final that night.

As he wandered round under the stands, he was congratulated by some British journalists and confessed "I have to admit it was a great achievement for me." Quite out of character, at that time, he went on to forecast, quietly and rather shyly, "I'll go faster in the final!"

Getting the tickets was a bit of a problem. In fact, it was necessary to go right to the top of swimming, to Dr. Harold Henning, at that time honorary secretary of F.I.N.A. (the International Amateur Swimming Federation). The kind American managed to "find" a couple for Harry and Jean Wilkie.

The final on September 2nd had Taguchi, as the fastest qualifier, lined up in lane 4 with Wilkie (lane 5) and Hencken (lane 3) on either side of him. Another American, Rick Colella, the 1971 Pan-American champion, was next to David (lane 6).

Although neither Hencken nor Wilkie knew it at the time, the two great rivals of that moment and of the future, were about to set the pattern of their racing which was to be repeated many times, in many places.

Hencken swam it hard at the start and Wilkie came back at him over the second 100 metres. On this occasion, the more experienced American stormed into the lead, to turn after one lap (31.55 sec.)

already two metres ahead of East Germany's Klaus Katzur and Taguchi, with Wilkie (33.45 sec.) and Colella (33.49 sec.), separated by a whisker, in fifth and sixth positions and nearly three metres in arrears.

Collela made his move on the second length and had pulled himself up to second place by the 100 metres mark where he touched in 1 min. 10.31 sec. But Hencken was holding his pace and his place and with 1 min. 8.34 sec. was still two seconds ahead of the field.

At this stage Igor Cherdakov of the Soviet Union had moved just ahead of Katzur to take third place, Taguchi had dropped back to fifth and Wilkie (1 min. 11.37 sec.) was sixth, four metres behind Hencken. With one lap to go, Hencken still held his dominating lead and was almost three metres ahead and Colella, Wilkie and Taguchi were bunched together in that order.

The final 50 metres was a foregone conclusion for Hencken, who became Olympic champion in a World and Games record of 2 min. 21.55 sec. The surprise was that Wilkie and Taguchi covered the last lap almost as quickly as Hencken — in fact, the Scot was only six hundredths of a second slower and the Japanese seven hundredths.

Wilkie's final 2 min. 23.67 sec. for European and Commonwealth records, gave him the silver. Taguchi (2 min. 23.88 sec.) was slightly slower than in his heat and had to settle for the bronze. The fading Colella (2 min. 24.28 sec.) was fourth.

David couldn't have won his out-of-the-blue medal at a better time, or on a better day. It had been one disaster after another for the British swimming team and here, at last, they had a medal. But it was more than that . . . it was Harry Wilkie's birthday and what a great present David gave his father.

Yes, young Wilkie had done better than the greatest expectations. Yet there was one man, at least, and a very knowledgeable one, who was convinced that David could have done even better, that he could have won. That man was Don Talbot, one of the world's leading coaches, who was in charge of the Australian team in Munich.

Talbot was convinced then and reiterated his belief many times after that the Scot was beaten by inexperience and not by Hencken. Talbot was sure that had Wilkie started to race with greater authority in his swimming and attacked more in the early stages he would have come out with the gold medal.

The man-to-man analysis, though perhaps boy-to-boy would be more apt for both were only 18 at the time, illustrates Talbot's line of thinking. Hencken's lap splits were 31.55, 36.79, 37.01 and 36.20 sec. Wilkie did 33.45, 37.92, 36.04 and 36.26 sec. So, the Scot's first lap deficit of 1.94 sec. had become only 2.12 sec. by the finish and who knows what he might have achieved in that race if he had not let Hencken get away so far from him at the beginning. Equally, had he put the pressure on at the start, he might have died at the end as Colella did.

David's reflective thoughts about Munich as the place where he began to mature and get confidence in himself may be quite true. But he wasn't as sure of himself then as he imagined. Looking back, David had to admit:

"I did not have enough confidence in myself in Munich to swim the race the way Hencken swam his, to go out hard and hold on. I had to go out slow and then come back hard, because I really didn't know what I was capable of doing. After qualifying for the final, I knew I had a chance of a medal and wasn't prepared to take risks."

All this — the Talbot theory, the Wilkie wonderings, the speculation and the split times — are academic now. On his pre-Games form he had no business to win a medal. On his attitude in the years leading up to Munich Wilkie might say, in all honesty, he did not deserve one. But on the day he did and that is the firm fact, recorded in history. As usual, David is generous in acknowledging the part other people have played in his successes. And his Munich silver was no exception.

"I had a lot of faith in the team coach Hammy Bland. He was in charge of me for the 12 weeks leading up to my first big moment and I was very pleased with what he did for me. He took me in a short time from being a not very good swimmer to second in the Olympics and he must take a lot of the acclaim for that."

The compliment will be appreciated by Bland, who received more kicks than kind words after Britain's bad showing in 1972.

Wilkie had two more events in Munich, but neither were significant. He had the twelfth fastest time (2 min. 13.25 sec.) in the heats of the 200 metres medley on September 3rd and, the following day, helped the squad of Colin Cunningham, John Mills and Malcolm Windeatt through the heats and to a British-best time and seventh place in the final of the 4 x 100 metres medley relay.

It was the end of the first chapter of success. Suddenly the Scot was a hot property. Americans stopped saying "Who's this guy Wilkie? . . . Never heard of him." Now, they were asking "Where's he going? Florida? California? . . . Is he coming to us?" And the short answer was "Yes".

6

1973

BELGRADE

. . . and the first world title and record

Life began, for the third time, in January 1973 when Wilkie went to the University of Miami, Florida, on a full scholarship, to study marine biology — and, with his Munich medal providing the spur, to try to become a great swimmer.

For David, who has always thought of his life being split into separate phases, of Ceylon followed by Scotland, it was like being born again. It was back to the days of sunshine and palm trees, the warm ocean and the fish, yet with a new purpose. No more the cold and chill of winter, no more shivering at early morning training and no more reluctance to do his swimming thing. Wilkie, always a realist, had come to recognise that he did have competitive ambitions and that he had been given a splendid chance to realise them.

"The time I spent in Miami before the World championships in Belgrade was very important. I was getting training I had never had before, in ideal conditions in the open air and I was having competition nearly every week against people who were more than capable of beating me. There were a lot of factors that helped me along. I found I had a desire to better myself, to prove something to myself . . . to find out if I could be a really good swimmer.

"My main aim was to beat John Hencken in the 200 metres breaststroke at the World championships to avenge my defeat in Munich — and beat everybody else as well. And I wanted to break a world record — John's if possible. It had been a dream of mine to hold a world record, as far back even as when I started swimming, but I had never really taken the dream seriously."

What a contrary devil! He didn't want to be involved . . . he refused to be involved . . . he had to be driven to be involved. Yet, deep down, he had been dreaming of breaking World swimming records!

Staying in America from the end of the university year in early May until July posed financial problems for David. His scholarship did not cover his living costs during vacations and Miami is not a cheap place. But he decided to manage as best he could and he was helped by an invitation to swim in California, at the big Santa Clara club international meeting, in the third week of June. Typically, they were kind enough to put him up for three weeks and let him train with the club. It was a great help.

It was during his first half-year in America that David began to think about the 200 metres medley — that test of the complete swimmer, involving fifty metre legs on butterfly, backstroke, breast-stroke and front crawl — as well as his individual breaststroke events. Wilkie even confessed to doing quite well on it.

So he was in good all-round shape when he returned to Britain in time to take part in the national championships in Coventry in August after which the team for Belgrade would be announced. He got an immediate chance to test his front crawl in the Warrender squad for the club 4 x 100 metres freestyle relay. It was the first time teams from outside England had been allowed to take part in relay events at this meeting, organised by the Amateur Swimming Association (of England) yet traditionally recognised as the British championships.

The Warrender quartet put up the fastest heat time of the 24 teams, 3 min. 46.9 sec., which would have been a Scottish record, except that they were disqualified for a faulty take-over. The men involved were the incoming Wilson Mills and the outgoing Wilkie.

There are some who believe that a "flyer" can be blamed as much on the incoming swimmer, for not coming into the wall correctly, as the outgoing man for going too quickly. A take-over is a two-way partnership, of split-second, precision timing and each partner has to be absolutely spot-on in what he is doing.

Wilkie, by now used to the slick American take-over techniques, did not allow for the comparatively slower approach to the wall of Mills and was more speedily away from his mark than he should have been. And it was all so unnecessary, for Warrender could have been 8½ seconds slower and still got into the final. There were no mistakes though in the medley relay in which, thanks to David's fine breaststroke leg, Warrender took the silver medals behind Southampton.

David snatched second place, behind Brian Brinkley, in the 200 metres medley (2 min. 12.96 sec.) by four hundredths of a second from Southampton's Ray Terrell. He won the 100 metres breaststroke (1 min. 7.88 sec.) by half a metre from Sunderland's Paul Naisby, with David Leigh of Sheffield close-by in third place.

He retained his 200 metres breaststroke title (2 min. 27.60 sec.) in beating Malcolm O'Connell of Southampton by nearly three seconds. And he rounded off four busy days by coming second in the 100 metres freestyle (55.79 sec.) behind yet another Southampton swimmer, Colin Cunningham, and ahead of his American-born, Scottish and Warrender team-mate Gordon Downie. It all boded well for Belgrade.

But there was an underlying feeling of tension at the championships which exploded to the surface as soon as the World championships team had been announced. Perhaps to teach the swimmers a lesson for their dreadful showing — Wilkie apart — at the Munich Olympics, the selectors decided on a tough policy for the big event of 1973.

They stipulated that, to earn selection, individual swimmers or relay squads must have equalled or bettered the times of the last placed finalists in Munich, since April 1st, 1973. On the face of it, this was not an unreasonable demand.

But when the team were announced, it became clear that the selectors were implementing their policy to the ultimate. They refused to allow any member of the World championships squad to take part in any event in Belgrade for which they had not done the British qualifying time. The result was heart-break all round.

This rigid, unyielding, almost savage attitude towards the cream of the swimming youth in Britain meant that four of the 11 who went to Yugoslavia were only permitted to race in relays . . . it meant that Brinkley, the mainstay of the home-based international team, was not allowed to compete in the 400 metres freestyle — the event for which he had taken fifth place in Munich! . . . that Terrell, who *had* done a target time for the 200 metres medley but could not swim this in Belgrade because he was Britain's No. 3 (and countries were limited to two) was restricted to one relay appearance.

Team manager Alan Clarkson made two appeals to the selectors to relax their stringent attitude. Once the swimmers were in Belgrade, super-fit and raring to go after two weeks of ideal training there, it seemed to everyone that not to let them all have the benefit that could have come from racing against the best competitors in the world, was a thoroughly dog-in-the-manger attitude and completely unjustified.

Clarkson's last ditch appeal brought a terse three word refusal, "No other additions", and bitter disappointment for officials and competitors alike. So, many of the squad had to sit on the benches, frustrated and angry, watching inferior rivals take part in events from which they had been excluded needlessly.

Wilkie was the one member of the team not put under tension by the selection policies. He had beaten his three target times during the Coca-Cola International at Crystal Palace in April with 1 min. 6.36 sec. for 100 metres breaststroke, 2 min. 27.44 sec. for 200 metres breaststroke and 2 min. 10.0 sec. for 200 metres medley.

On their way to Belgrade, the men's team detoured to East Berlin to take part in the Europa Cup against the top European nations — East Germany, the Soviet Union, West Germany, Hungary, France, Sweden and Poland — on August 18th and 19th.

David, with his divided loyalties, caused some alarm by indicating that he would prefer to swim in the Scottish championships in Edinburgh rather than go to the Iron Curtain meeting. Finally, it was decided he would compete in the early part of the Scottish event and then travel out with the Europa Cup squad.

It took 14 hours to get to Berlin and the stresses showed in the Cup contest as the Britons struggled to beat their rivals under the handicap of trying, at the same time, to take this last chance of doing World qualifying times. That they managed to avoid relegation was a feat in itself and it took some outspoken driving by coach David Haller to bring about that result.

Even Wilkie was nervous and edgy as he waited for the start of his first race, the 100 metres breaststroke. He took a long time to bend down into his start position, causing two other swimmers to fall into the water and he was reprimanded by the referee.

Swimming on the other side of the bath, away from the main action, he had to settle for third place behind West Germany's Walter Kusch and Russia's Mikhail Kriukin and his 1 min. 7.1 sec. was eight tenths of a second outside his best 1973 time.

On the second day, in the 200 metres breaststroke, Wilkie let Kriukin get too far ahead on the first two laps and though he was closing very fast at the end, he could manage only to finish second in 2 min. 26.08 sec.

The setting for swimming's first World championships was perfect at the Tasmajdan pool, in the centre of Belgrade; the sun shone and for most of the 14 days before the competitions began the British team had the place to themselves and all the water time they needed.

David had trained hard and was in good shape for Belgrade and the final two weeks of preparation were the best he had ever experienced.

"I was looking forward to some interesting races, especially with John Hencken, and when I only came fourth in the 100 metres breaststroke I was a bit disappointed. I thought I would have done better than that."

Wilkie qualified for this final as the sixth fastest, having won his heat in 1 min. 6.98 sec. But Hencken, in winning the last of five pre-liminaries, had set a world record of 1 min. 4.35 sec. Also through to the final were the Olympic champion Nobutaka Taguchi of Japan (1:5.80), the European champion Nikolay Pankin of Russia (1:6.10), America's Rick Colella (1:6.72) and Kriukin (1:6.78).

In the final, on September 4th, David set out to try and stay with the fast-sprinting Hencken — not the Scot's normal racing procedure — and he paid dearly for the change in tactics over the last length. In the end he was edged into fourth place by Taguchi as Kriukin chased Hencken for the gold and Pankin and Colella tussled for fifth and sixth. The American won in another world record of 1 min. 4.02 sec. while the Russian set European figures of 1 min. 4.61 sec. For Wilkie there was the satisfaction of a Commonwealth mark of 1 min. 5.74 sec., seven hundredths behind the Japanese. But no medal.

"I was a bit despondent after that and it didn't give me all that confidence for the 200 metres which was to be held two days later. But the race came and the heat was most important for me because I was just off John's world record and I knew then that I was capable of winning the final and breaking the record.

"I remember as I was warming up for the final hearing that Gudrun Wegner of East Germany had broken the world record in the 400 metres medley (actually she was the first girl to go under five minutes). And I thought to myself 'David, there is no reason why you can't do that too in the next race'. I really was aiming for that world time and was very confident I could do it."

Wilkie improved his European and Commonwealth records (his silver medal-winning time in Munich) by 2.7 sec. to 2 min. 20.94 sec. in beating Russia's Igor Cherdakov by six metres in heat two. This was only 0.32 of a second outside the world figures that Hencken had set during the U.S. trials in Louisville thirteen days earlier. And from heat four the American emerged as the only challenger to the Scot with a 2 min. 21.50 sec. Now it was confrontation . . . now it was two men battling for supremacy and only one could win.

The race pattern went as it had in Munich. Hencken stormed away and turned at 100 metres in 1 min. 6.78 sec., nearly two seconds faster than his 'spilt' the year before. Wilkie was in third place, but his 1 min 7.56 sec. was almost four seconds better than his Olympic effort. The American was still ahead at the 150 metre turn, then the Scot made his planned challenge. With surging powerful strokes Wilkie edged ahead of the tiring Hencken to win by inches in 2 min. 19.28 sec., a world record (and, of course, European, Commonwealth, British and Scottish ones too). Hencken, with 2 min. 19.95 sec., was also inside his previous best time.

> "I was delirious, shocked out of my mind to think I had broken the world record. Then they raised the Union Jack and played God Save the Queen. Suddenly I realised all the Aussies and Canadians were singing. I had been thrilled by the record, now I was touched emotionally. To me it was a rare display of traditional Empire unity. It is a moment I won't forget."

So, there was David, world champion and world record-holder, thrilled and excited, with his desires, for the moment, fulfilled. And there, in front of him, was another golden target, one that was within his reach if he had given it any serious thought, the 200 metres medley.

The first seed in this event was Stan Carper of the United States on the strength of his U.S. trials time of 2 min. 8.88 sec. And, on paper, the No. 7 was Olympic champion Gunnar Larsson of Sweden, whose form was suspect and who had only managed a fifth place in the Europa Cup with 2 min. 14.5 sec. compared with his Munich-winning world record of 2 min. 7.17 sec.

The big, fair-haired, square-shouldered Larsson had put on a tremendous amount of weight after the 1972 Games and though he had managed to trim off most of the surplus for Belgrade, there was more than a hint of fat over the muscle and his 1973 times were not particularly good. Already he was preoccupied with his future career and whether he would retire from competition.

Even the partisan Swedish officials were worried. They had not entered him for the second of his Olympic gold medal events, the 400 metres medley, in order to conserve his energies for this one race. Knowing that breaststroke is the key to the medley, they were even more worried after seeing Wilkie in action against Hencken.

Wilkie won his heat on September 7th in a Commonwealth record of 2 min. 9.61 sec. and only Andras Hargitay of Hungary, the Olympic 400 metres medley bronze medallist, went faster . . . seven hundredths of a second faster, in fact. Larsson (2:10.13) and Carper (2:11.04) qualified for the final that night as fourth and fifth best.

Medley races are always exciting to watch because fortunes fluctuate according to the strength of each individual on each of the four strokes involved — and this applies even at top level, where the swimmers must be good all-rounders, yet are still inclined to be better at some strokes than the others. And this certainly applied in the Belgrade final.

Carper was the only one of the eight finalists to "split" at under a minute (59.69 sec.) after the butterfly and backstroke legs. Hargitay was just ahead of Larsson, but a metre behind the American at this stage and Wilkie was trailing (1 min. 2.07 sec.) in seventh place as he touched, or rather crashed into the wall on his turn from backstroke to breaststroke.

He recovered as quickly as he could and ate into the deficit on his famed breaststroke and fought like fury over the closing 50 metres on front crawl. But he had to settle for the bronze medal and a Commonwealth record of 2 min. 8.84 sec.

Larsson, who began to feel the pain around 125 metres but just put his head down and kept going, demonstrated the courage that had won him those two golds in Munich the year before by snatching the World title from Carper by less than a tenth of a second (2:8.36) and beating the Scot by 0.48 of a second. Wilkie had no one to blame except himself for not winning that gold and he was the first to admit it.

"It was my own stupid fault. If I come up to the wall on my right hand on that change then I have to do a somersault turn, which I don't like doing. So I tried to come up on my left hand on the backstroke and do a grab turn and I misjudged it. (What he did was to get much too close to the bath end, crash his arm and then his head on the wall.) And if I hadn't done that I probably could have won in around 2 min. 7.9 sec.

"I suppose my ambitions in Belgrade had ended after the 200 metres breaststroke, that I hadn't really prepared mentally properly for the medley and was looking on it as a bonus instead of a serious event. I was very pleased to come third in the final. I had never thought I would be that high anyway. Also, even if I hadn't done that bad turn, things might have worked in aggregate just the same, because after that mistake I was very angry with myself and really pushed the breaststroke and front crawl coming home. If I hadn't been so annoyed I might not have pushed so hard."

There were suggestions, though not by Wilkie, that David's tinted goggles — fine for the natural sun-lit days but, perhaps, not so good under flood-lit nights — could have caused the turning trouble. British coach Dave Haller would not accept this theory. His view, quietly and firmly put, was: "I believe David just did not give himself enough warming-up time to think out his medley race in detail before the start, as he did on Thursday when he won the 200 metres breaststroke."

Peter Daland, the United States 1972 Olympic team coach, who was in Belgrade just for his sheer love of swimming, was a little more charitable. He was also extremely prophetic: "The goggles may have caused Wilkie's turning mess-up. But the boy has unlimited talent. He has proved it here and he is going to be one of the world's greatest swimmers in 1976 when he goes to the Montreal Olympics."

Again, the Scot's closing race was the 4 x 100 metres medley relay. He pulled the British team from seventh to third with a breaststroke split of 1 min. 5.71 sec. but the squad dropped back again to finish seventh in 3 min. 59.04 sec., a fraction slower than their timing for the same placing in Munich. Predictably, only one man swam the relay breaststroke leg faster (1:3.55) than Wilkie. His name? John Hencken! Of course. But that is a recurring story.

There was one more honour to follow for David Wilkie before the next chapter in his swimming story. In the New Years honours list of 1974, David Andrew Wilkie was the recipient of an M.B.E. for his services to his sport.

7

1974

CHRISTCHURCH

The golden gremlins appear

Travel, multiplied by tiredness, equals toil and adds up to trouble. This equation should have been transparently clear to Wilkie early in 1974 when he set off from Miami to take part in his second Commonwealth Games, in Christchurch, New Zealand.

By this stage, David was not a novice competitor and certainly not an inexperienced traveller. Many journeys between Ceylon and Britain, to the United States, Canada, South Africa and different parts of Europe should have made him aware of the effects of air travel, jet lag and time changes. In fact, the penny was only just beginning to drop.

"It was around this time that I was beginning to realise just what was involved and how much travelling was taking out of me. I think it must have taken me 36 hours to get to New Zealand. This included a six-hour stop-over in Australia and that was tiring in itself. By the time I got to Christchurch, there was also an eight-hour time change to contend with. On top of which I arrived after the rest of the Scottish team — and that was a mistake."

These were not the only snags. If they had been the remedy would have been fairly simple — get to New Zealand earlier. But Coach Diaz in Miami had not wanted David to take part at all. So far as pro-American Diaz was concerned, the United States were not in the Commonwealth, they were not in the Games, therefore the Commonwealth Games were not important. Anyway, David had his training and his university studies to do.

After Belgrade and his first World title and record, Wilkie had taken a break from swimming and did not get back into training until the start of November.

"We had two weeks in Jamaica in December and though Coach really wasn't too happy about me going to New Zealand, he wasn't going to stop me. Still it meant taking four weeks off from very important training and my university classes.

"But I was determined to go. I wanted to swim for Scotland. Even though I knew I wouldn't be in tip-top condition, I thought I would be in good enough shape to win three races. I never expected David Leigh or Paul Naisby (his English rivals) would swim so well. The way things turned out, I wasn't fit enough to handle the travel, I should have arrived earlier, and I hadn't done any special preparations for the races."

To continue the saga, David also turned up in Christchurch with back trouble, which he tried to play down and many people attempted to play up to the extent that he would have to quit swimming. Between the two extremes, Wilkie had to admit he did have a back injury and that it was causing him pain and hampering his training.

The trouble started in November 1973, during training, but Wilkie did not realise the pain was coming from a slipped vertebra in his upper back, between his shoulder blades. He did not seek treatment for a month, by which time the muscles around the spine also had become misplaced. Though the vertebra could easily be manipulated into place, it was as quick to go out again, particularly under stress, because the muscles holding it had not had time to reform into their correct position. This, too, had cost David vital training time and affected his fitness . . . but nothing was important except being in New Zealand to swim for Scotland.

On the previous year's times, David should have won the 100 and 200 metres breaststroke and 200 metres medley titles without going into top gear. He was the Commonwealth record-holder for 100 metres in 1 min. 5.74 sec., almost two seconds faster than Australia's Nigel Cluer, with Leigh and Naisby yet to break 1 min. 8 sec.

For the 200 metres breaststroke, his 2:19.28 world record in Belgrade was six and a half seconds inside Cluer's 1974 best, Leigh was four seconds slower and Naisby did not rank in the Commonwealth top six. For the medley, the closest man was Brian Brinkley, and his English record of 2:10.95 was more than two seconds slower than David's Scottish, British and Commonwealth figures. So, who was worrying?

Wilkie's Christchurch programme was:

Friday, January 25th: 400 metres medley (heats) and 4 x 100 metres freestyle (final).
Saturday, January 26th: 200 metres breaststroke (heats).
Monday, January 28th: 200 metres medley (heats).
Wednesday, January 30th: 200 metres medley (final) in the afternoon and 200 metres breaststroke (final) in the evening.
Thursday, January 31st: 100 metres breaststroke (heats).
Friday, February 1st: 100 metres breaststroke (final) in the afternoon and the 4 x 100 metres medley relay (final) as the last swimming event of the Games in the evening.

It was a heavy stint, yet possible to complete in good order for, unlike the Olympics, there would be no pressure in heats in order to qualify for finals, for the standards in the Commonwealth Games do not have strength in depth.

David paddled through the long medley, not looking too sparkling — but then it isn't really his race — to finish 12th out of 14 competitors. And Scotland came fourth in the freestyle sprint relay.

"I didn't begin to feel even half myself until after the heats of the 200 metres breaststroke on the Saturday and if the final had been the same day, instead of on the following Wednesday, I never would have won. I was very lucky there were four days in between."

Leigh took the first heat in a Games record of 2 min. 26.29 sec. and was followed in by Naisby (2:27.54). Defending champion Bill Mahony of Canada, behind whom Wilkie had finished in third place four years earlier, won the second preliminary in 2:28.09 with Australia's Cluer only just behind. Scotland's David came second in the third with 2:30.79 and went into the final as the sixth best. This wasn't sizzling form by the World champion by any stretch of imagination.

Sunday was a real day of rest for everyone since there were no competitions. On Monday, there were two heats of the 200 metres medley. Gary MacDonald of Canada set a Games record in the first in 2 min. 12.91 sec. and Wilkie snatched the second by fifteen hundredths of a second from England's Ray Terrell, having turned a half-distance deficit of 1.77 sec. into victory thanks to a fine third leg on breaststroke.

This hopping from one event to another and then back again is a peculiarity of the Commonwealth Games programming and while it may have given Wilkie time to find his form before the races that mattered, it is not the normal system. At all other major championships — Olympics, Worlds and Europeans — heats and finals of an event are completed in the same day, except if there are semi-finals or in the 800 metres for women and 1,500 metres for men when the finals are the day immediately following the preliminaries.

After another day of rest from racing for all the swimmers, Wilkie faced up to two finals on the Wednesday — the medley in the afternoon and the breaststroke in the evening. There was no messing around now. David and Terrell swam the first half of the medley to touch almost level, then the Scot, inevitably, opened up a winning gap on breaststroke and front-crawled home to win by 2.62 sec. from England's Brinkley, who had turned fourth at 100 metres but produced one of his renowned last-lap sprints to take the silver.

Wilkie's 2 min. 10.11 sec. for his first Commonwealth title, was a Games record and MacDonald prevented a Scotland-England sweep-up of medals by edging Terrell into fourth place. David had expected that the medley, with its great threat from Brinkley, would be his toughest race. In fact, the Wilkie programme became progressively more difficult from then on.

The Scot was only narrowly ahead of Leigh and Naisby at half-distance in the 200 metres breaststroke confrontation and had to fight extremely hard to hold off the determined closing challenge of Leigh, though Naisby was trailing away into third place.

Wilkie just won, by 0.33 sec., in a Games record of 2:24.42, nearly two seconds faster than David of England had done in the heats, but five seconds outside his own world record. It was a close squeak and, certainly, spice was added to the 100 metres battle to come.

"No one should have been able to beat me in the 200 metres breaststroke, but in my state of tiredness and especially after seeing them in the heats, I knew I was going to have a good race with David and Paul. In all the circumstances, I was very happy to win two golds in the same day.

"I should have gone straight to bed, instead of doing some interviews, for I needed the rest. If I had, maybe the 100 metres might

Wilkie with his Warrender club coach and friend Frank Thomas

David the boy, in 1970, chasing Canada's Bill Mahony in the Commonwealth Games 200 metres breaststroke final in Edinburgh and David the man, in 1975, on the way to retaining his World 200 metres crown in Cali, Colombia.

have been a different story. As it was, David Leigh beat me . . . he swam a good race and I swam a bad one. I did all the work the first 50 metres and David came at me on the second and I had nothing to hold him off with. It was lucky that Paul (who was third again) didn't come a lot harder as well."

Wilkie's memory was right. Leigh, who had been psyched up to a new high to beat the Scot by the Master of Psych himself, Dave Haller, on this occasion coach to the English team, was level with Wilkie at the 50 metres turn. Then the battle really was joined and from halfway down the last length of the pool it was Leigh who produced that little extra when it counted to defeat his more fancied rival and stop Wilkie's golden hat-trick.

There was one unfortunate complication which affected all the 100 metres finalists. The start was delayed for 25 minutes so that the Queen could see the race for which it had been agreed she would present the medals. Yet though it made an unforgettable Royal occasion, officials had overlooked the effect the wait would have on the competitors.

All their warming-up was wasted as they waited to be called to the starting blocks. Even the ice-calm Leigh — "Cool hand Luke" to his team-mates — admitted he would have preferred to have raced first, then waited to receive his medal from Her Majesty.

As Wilkie said afterwards: "Having warmed up and loosened up, I could feel my muscles tightening again as we waited. But that's a bad excuse (for losing) and I'm not going to make it, because it was the same for everyone."

Bad excuse or not, the delay must have had a similar effect on all eight finalists, even if it only heightened the normal pre-race tension, though that can hardly be measured in medal colour.

This defeat was significant for Wilkie in a way which did not become clear until a later stage in his career. It marked the first appearance of David's golden gremlins, who somehow contrived to make him fall at the third hurdle when triple successes were so close as to be near certainties.

8

1974

VIENNA

Gold and Silver — but no waltz

Whenever anyone mentions Vienna there is an automatic response in David Wilkie's memory. Not for him the romantic musical visions of Strauss, the Blue Danube and Tales of the Vienna Woods . . . though the Gold and Silver Waltz may strike a responsive chord.

For David, recalling the Austrian capital means the European championships there in August 1974, conjures up a two gold and a silver medal symphony and a chapter in a horror story with the hero caught up in a nightmarish sequence leading to disaster, all of his own making. That he was triumphant in the end does not — and never will — erase the blot from Wilkie's copybook.

What David did was to stop swimming, thinking a false start had been signalled, when he should have kept going. It was an action of classic stupidity . . . the elementary mistake of a novice in his first race and not the instant reaction of a World champion with a wealth of high-level competitive experience.

It was Wilkie's first event of the championships, staged in the open-air Prater pool on the outskirts of Vienna. And there was nothing special, no warning uneasiness, about the start of heat 2 of the 100 metres breaststroke. The men dived in, surfaced — and Wilkie stopped dead.

As British fans and team-mates screeched in alarm, and his other four rivals sped down the pool, David turned to go back to the start, then turned back again to see the rest of the field racing away from him as he impotently waved his arms in the air, trying to attract the attention of the race officials.

His rivals were well into their strokes and up to 15 metres ahead of him before Wilkie finally realised there wasn't going to be a recall and, from a standstill, static position in the water tried to get going again. It was a situation for Superman and, sadly, facts are different from fiction. Wilkie did restart, but he did not win. His official time of 1 min. 14.79 sec. was the slowest of the 23 competitors, seven seconds behind the eighth and last qualifier for the final and nine seconds outside his own best. And he could have gone through without even going into top gear!

In fact, what David mistook for a false start signal was a klaxon in the noisy crowd and British team manager Alan Clarkson protested along those lines . . . there had been an apparent false start, with the impression being given that the competitors had been recalled. The jury of appeal rejected that plea. The result stood. And David, though in obvious distress at this shattering experience, could blame nobody but himself.

He sat, in tears, after the jury's decision and coach Dave Haller had to walk him up and down in the gardens behind the pool to bring David back to accepting that what had been done was done.

"I thought that I and Wolfram Sperling of East Germany, in the next lane, had taken flyers. So when I heard the klaxon I thought it was an official recall. And even when Wolfram hesitated and then went on, I couldn't believe the officials would let the race proceed.

"I should have won that 100. Looking back at my 'split' later, in the medley relay, I should have been a certainty to win it. But I didn't and that whole incident kicked my confidence for the 200 out of the door.

"In the morning heats of the 200, four days later, I felt bad and I did a poor time (David did 2:24.37, the second fastest and not so bad!). And I was very concerned about the final, which is why I swam it the way I did . . . just to win, without worrying about a world record."

The most interesting aspect of that Wilkie victory was the tactical battle. He and team-mate David Leigh, who had swum into third place in the 100 metres final in Wilkie's unfortunate absence, knew the danger man would be Russia's Nikolay Pankin, the 100 metres European champion of 1970 and 1974 and 200 metres silver medallist in 1970. The British plan was to hold the race back and not let the Russian use them as pace-makers.

Pankin, sandwiched between the Britons, fell for their ploy. After two lengths of unhurried though powerful strokes, there was only 1.53 sec. between the leading six with Wilkie (1 min. 11.29 sec.) and Leigh (1:11.69) in fifth and sixth places, Pankin lying third (1:11.23) and Austria's Steffen Kriechbaum, setting a lunatic pace for him (1:10.16), just ahead.

Then it was time for Wilkie to go and he did just that, covering the second half of his race two seconds faster than the first, for a comfortable three and a half metres victory over the Russian. Leigh picked up another bronze and had the satisfaction of setting an English record of 2:23.79.

Wilkie's gold medal-winning 2:20.42 was only 1.14 sec. outside his own year-old world mark and it sent him, with new good heart, into his challenge for his third event, the 200 metres medley.

"My medley had improved in the past year and I'd done well in the N.C.A.A. (fourth in the 200 yards in 1 min. 52.71 sec.), which converted very close to the long-course world record. And as I am a better swimmer in a 50 metre pool than a 25 yard or metres one I knew if I could hit that form in Vienna it would be right on for the record.

"I did a very good heat (2 min. 8.48 sec., a British record and just over a second outside the world and European figures of Olympic champion Gunnar Larsson of Sweden). But I knew I had a tough fight on my hands with Christian Lietzmann of East Germany. He didn't have a weakness on any of his strokes and as he had qualified second to me from the heats (2:8.71) after coming second in the 400 metres medley the day before, he was the man to beat.

"Lietzmann took it out very fast indeed on butterfly and backstroke, but he knew I was going to be coming at him after the 100 metres turn, on breaststroke. So he really had to push to try to keep ahead of me and it must have been disheartening for him to feel me catching him up, even though he was expecting it. So, psychologically, it was a blow when I was there . . . and worse when I passed him. He started to tire on freestyle and I could feel it. So I kicked really hard on the last 25 metres.

"I was so excited then, because I realised the world record must be on and I could feel myself getting stronger . . . adrenalin force I suppose, I don't think I have ever come home as hard as I did that day and I finished in 2 min. 6.32 sec. and beat the world record by 0.85 sec. It was great and I think that 200 metres medley was one of the finest races I've ever swum."

That performance made David a double world record holder. But the glory lasted for less than half a day for, away to the west in Concord, California, the U.S. National A.A.U. championships were taking place. And on the day David won the European medley, his perennial rival John Hencken was winning the 200 metres breast-stroke title in 2 min. 18.93 sec., to shave thirty-five hundredths of a second from Wilkie's world time.

Eight days later, America's Steve Furniss equalled David's world medley record in Concord, during the U.S.-East Germany match. It was amazing that such a thing could happen . . . on the other side of the world . . . to equal the precise time to a hundredth of a second.

"Steve swims a very different race to me. He does the first 100 metres hard and the second less so, while I do the second 100 faster than the first. So to come out with the same result is pretty interesting."

Yet the Vienna medal that pleased David most was the silver he won as a member of Britain's 4 x 100 metres medley relay squad.

"This proved to be one of Britain's greatest relay teams ever put together. I think it was a fantastic swim by all the lads in the team — we never really expected to get second even though we knew it was a possibility. But we could have come as low as fourth or fifth for there were some very powerful teams, including West Germany, the favourites, East Germany, the defending champions, and Russia.

"All our team really got down to the job in hand and all produced their best times. Colin Cunningham led off on back-stroke and became the first Briton to go under the minute with 59.82 sec., which was a great swim for him. I went next and had my personal best breaststroke split (1 min. 3.61 sec.) and we had pulled from fifth to second.

"Steve Nash went in and swam a hell of a 'fly. I guess Steve was supposed to be the weak link in the squad, but he proved to be just as strong as the others. And although we had dropped to third behind West Germany and East Germany, who had the European 100 metres butterfly champion Roger Pyttel in their team, we were not far behind and we were still ahead of Russia.

"Brian Brinkley on freestyle had to hold off Vladimir Bure, Russia's European sprint champion, and try to catch Wilfried Hartung of East Germany. And he stood no nonsense from either of them and we came in second behind the West Germans.

"I remember looking up to the score board and muddling which lane we had been swimming in. And I groaned and said 'No! We're fourth!' But, in fact, I was looking at the time for the East Germans. Our lads were so elated and it was a job really well done."

David, rightly, gives credit to the whole team for winning Britain's first European relay medals since 1962, when a squad of Stan Clarke, Peter Kendrew, John Martin-Dye and Wilkie's hero Bobby McGregor took the silvers in the 4 x 100 metres freestyle in Leipzig.

But it was the inspiration and influence of David and Brian that raised Colin and Steve to a level they had never achieved before. Coach Dave Haller, preoccupied with the final of the 1,500 metres, in which Britain's Jimmy Carter was doing shoulder-to-shoulder battle with East Germany's Frank Pfuetze, could not give his full attention to the relay team.

Not until this 30-lap race was over, and Carter had been forced to settle for the silver, just nineteen hundredths of a second behind Pfuetze, could Haller start to think of Britain's next event. He looked around and found the quartet sitting quietly in a corner, with Wilkie and Brinkley doing the psyching-up job for him.

So, with two golds plus the relay silver to jingle, jangle on his way back to Miami, it could be said Wilkie was unlucky, again, not to have had a golden hat-trick to emulate the three gold medal success of his fellow-Scot Ian Black at the European championships of 1958 in Budapest.

Yet, in one respect, Wilkie was lucky to have swum in Vienna at all and if the British team had not, at last, acquired their own physiotherapist in the person of Tony Power, a former Olympic fencing representative, the Scot might not have done so.

According to Haller, Wilkie's back injury, which had plagued him in Christchurch at the start of the year, was extremely painful and daily training was difficult to say the least. "If it had not been for Tony, David would not have swum in Vienna" is Haller's view.

Power puts it a little less dramatically.

"I wouldn't say he couldn't have swum, but he would have had to swim with his performance impaired and in great discomfort. What David had was a prolapsed inter-vertebra disc in the thoracic spine (between the shoulder blades). This meant his spine was slightly out of true, i.e. he had a scoliosis (sideways curve) of the spine. It was, probably, an occupational hazard of a breaststroke swimmer, from wear and tear on the muscles under particular stress. It was a question of getting it straight and supple, by manipulation. But the area was very stiff even if there was no pain."

Power laid down a series of exercises, based on Yoga, to be done very slowly and designed just to move the injured part. He has kept an eye on David ever since their first meeting in Vienna and Wilkie has done the exercises religiously since that time.

9

1975

CALI

Handled with care

According to the Oxford Dictionary the original meaning of "Carnival" is a week of revelry and riotous amusement. The happy carnival city of Cali, Colombia, staged the second World championships in the summer of 1975, but though there was a certain amount of revelry for David Wilkie, in the celebration of his gold medal double, it was hardly a time of riotous amusement.

In fact, as Wilkie admits, 1975 was a funny-peculiar year for him . . . with training problems, experiments in technique, divided loyalties and travel complications that in the end were just too much. It was the year when he retained his World 200 metres breaststroke crown and won the 100 metres and then, as a favourite, failed even to qualify for the final of the 200 metres medley . . . when it was touch and go whether he would be fit to contest any of these three races . . . when British team coach Dave Haller had to call on every ounce of his instinct and knowledge to help Wilkie overcome the disastrous effects of a rash promise and an unwise journey.

But to go back to the early part of that year . . . David swam in the N.C.A.A. championships in Cleveland in March and was beaten by John Hencken into second place in both the 100 and 200 yards events, then got disqualified in the latter for using an illegal flutter kick on his fourth and fifth turns.

The next month David and his Miami coach Charlie Hodgson had a long talk about the dynamics of breaststroke and the fact that the leg kick moves the body faster through the water than the arms can pull it. With Montreal in mind, it was decided that David should change his large, long arm-pull to a wide, short, flat arm action with a very quick pull-back recovery.

Moment of triumph in Munich. A happy Wilkie receives his silver medal. His conqueror John Hencken of the United States proudly wears his gold. And a swimming rivalry that is to last four years begins.

Olympic baptism. Munich 1972 where 18-year-old David took second place in the 200 metres breaststroke for Britain's only swimming medal of the Games. Loosening up before the start of the final . . . away like an arrow at the gun . . . how David looked underwater on the way to his surprise silver.

Friends, team-mates and, on this occasion, rivals. Wilkie, of Scotland, wearing his Commonwealth Games 200 metres medley gold and England's runner-up, Brian Brinkley, with his silver.

With this change still in the difficult development stage after so many years of the old style, David returned home to swim for Scotland against Czechoslovakia and Hungary in Prague. His new-look technique took him to a Commonwealth record-equalling win in the 100 metres breaststroke in 1 min. 5.7 sec. He also took the 200 metres breaststroke and medley in unspectacular times by his standards.

David had decided to stay in Scotland to prepare for Cali, but after the World championships trials at Crystal Palace at the end of May, he went back to Miami.

"I wasn't getting enough competition and I wasn't happy with the way my training was going. I had three hard weeks with Charlie Raeburn (the Warrender club's new coach) but I missed the competitive element in work-outs and the open-air training in the sun."

Wilkie had agreed to swim for Scotland in an eight-nations meeting in Majorca in July, three weeks before the Cali swimming started. And although this now meant coming back across the Atlantic again, he stuck to his word.

"What I didn't realise was just how much the journey from Miami to Scotland, on to Majorca and then back to Cali would take out of me, even though we did have 17 days in Colombia before the swimming started.

"I had an obligation to Scotland to swim for them and although it wasn't an important match for me, it was important for our team and it would have been good if we could have won. But we didn't win, so it proved to be a bit of a wasted journey. I didn't swim well at all in Majorca, though I still won my races, but it was an interruption in my Cali preparations and it meant I got out there nearly a week after the rest of the British squad.

"What I didn't realise until later, at the end of the World championships in fact, was that I was so tired — more mentally than physically — after a busy week of travelling to and fro across the Atlantic, with two six-hour time changes."

So there was David, late in Cali, with a high pulse rate (indicating tiredness), still settling into his new stroke, and with vital work time lost during his Majorca mistake. Haller's tale of the following days makes harrowing reading. This is what Haller said:

"I let David hibernate for a few days, then started him on very long but easy swims, kicking, pulling and getting the feel of things. After a few days, as he had lost a lot of work-time because of the trip to Spain, I started to increase his training load.

"But after two days of this, he was obviously still very tired and any more training could have knocked him out. So we decided to put him back on light training once a day and when he wasn't doing this he was in bed.

"Technically, at this time, he didn't look very good in the water. His stroke was very uncoordinated, which was another indication of fatigue and he said he felt his legs were still very tired. Now breaststroke swimmers need to be very fresh to coordinate the stroke movements correctly and it is essential that the legs are working properly, for if this is wrong then there is a tendency to pull too quickly and mistime completely.

"So David rested as much as possible, and I kept checking his pulse, which wasn't going up so high on some swims and gradually he seemed to be recovering physically. Some days he swam well, some days terribly. In fact, there were more terrible days than good — about two bad to one good. So I rested him again and rested him more.

"I didn't over-sprint him and I didn't panic to try to get the best times out of him . . . or I tried not to. If he wanted to do a sprint and I didn't think it a good idea, then I didn't let him do it.

"A week before his first event he couldn't even break 32.5 sec. for 50 metres and David was going to need to be nearly two seconds faster on the first 50 metres of his 100 metres event and one second faster on the way to 200 metres. He didn't look good at all.

"However, he kept resting and gradually it all came together. He began to feel his legs working. His timing began to get right. His stroke began to coordinate. And with two days to the 100 metres breaststroke he looked much better."

It did not help when, five days before the opening of the championships, David fell a victim to the Cali collywobbles and lost seven pounds in weight as a result of his sharp 24-hour attack.

How did David react during these anxious weeks? Haller said:

"He was very very good about it, perhaps he was trying to hide his feelings, but I don't think so. He kept very relaxed and didn't get too upset, visibly anyway, and he didn't panic. He said 'if it happens, it happens'. Of course, David is a unique person. He has the strength of character and the courage to pull himself through something like this which is why he is such a great competitor."

David has similar opinions about Haller as a coach.

"Dave is very good when we come to the crunch, as we did in Colombia. He knows a lot about his swimmers. He has a great feel for the taper and that is the sign of the good coach. He has the taper technique down to a fine art and he has proved his worth over and over again, especially to me, ever since Belgrade."

Wilkie's first event, on Tuesday July 22nd, was the 100 metres, which, after the Vienna disaster, was tremendously important to him. He went through to the final as fifth fastest having won his morning heat in 1 min. 6.40 sec., just six hundredths faster than his team-mate David Leigh, the Commonwealth champion. And in the final, the same night, he beat the Olympic champion Nobutaka Taguchi of Japan by a body-length in 1 min. 4.26 sec., which was 1½ seconds faster than he had ever done before, with Leigh third in 1 min. 5.32 sec.

This Wilkie performance took 0.35 sec. off the European record of Russia's Mikhail Kriukin, who did not reach the final, and improved his own Commonwealth figures by 1.44 sec. The victory also eased the bitter memories of his Commonwealth Games defeat by Leigh the year before and his nightmarish lapse of concentration that had cost him the European title in Vienna.

The joyous relief of getting this one out of the way could be seen all over Wilkie's face and it set him on the way with supreme confidence for the defence of his 200 metres breaststroke two days later.

The Briton gave his rivals a taste of what was to come by heading the qualifiers with 2 min. 21.90 sec., one second faster than Pan-American champion Rick Colella, of the United States. And he swam majestically in the final to beat Colella by five metres in 2:18.23, the second fastest time of all time, a World championships, European and Commonwealth record and only two hundredths of a second outside the world record of the absent Hencken, who chose to miss the Cali event.

Colella, a generous loser, said afterwards:

"If it hadn't been for the conditions here (Cali is 3,000 feet above sea level and there were cold, strong head winds blowing down the pool) David would have been two seconds faster and broken the world record.''

But already the effects of Wilkie's pre-event exertions and brief illness were beginning to show. He was nothing like as sparkling at his second gold medal press conference as he had been at the first and Haller, team manager Alan Clarkson and doctor Dougie McIntyre were all too conscious of it and anxious to get their man home to bed as quickly as possible.

They had every reason, for in less than 10 hours, on the following morning, David had to be back at the pool, warming-up for his third gold medal attempt. This was in the 200 metres medley, an event in which he had the second fastest time ever to his credit. But instead of the expected comfortable 2 min. 10 sec. in the heats which would have taken him easily into the final, Wilkie could not get going from the start and he struggled home in 2 min. 12.68 sec., the ninth best, and eliminated from the final.

Wilkie was too true blue to blame anyone but himself.

"It was my fault and I did botch it up. I thought I could do my target time without trying and I hadn't taken anything else into account. Of course, earlier I had been so worried about my breast-stroke and more concerned about getting it right that I hadn't done any medley training.

"Still, I couldn't believe it at first. I really expected to get in there and I suppose I was one of the favourites to win. To be a favourite and not get into the final makes you feel you have let yourself and other people down. I felt very, very sad about that."

Indeed, Haller had confidently expected David to break the world medley record in the final and so had many of the American team coaches.

One more medal came Wilkie's way in Cali — to bring his total tally to three gold and two bronze medals from two World championships. That was in the 4×100 metres medley relay in which, thanks to his fine 1 min. 3.49 sec. breaststroke leg, which pulled the team up from seventh place to third, Britain took the bronzes.

"The times I did in the breaststroke were very pleasing indeed and if the conditions had been better I could have broken both of John's world records. That would have been great for me and set me up even more for Montreal.

"It was a bit upsetting to be so very close. It tends to make you think 'if I had done this turn a little bit quicker' . . . 'if I had not taken so long during that point of the race' . . . 'done a little bit more' . . . who knows? But this is not being realistic. Your time at the end of a race is the total result of all the effort you have put in from the start and you can't say that doing a bit more at one stage would have made any difference to the aggregate.

"I enjoyed Colombia. I think it was good for me to win those breaststroke races there and it was a good preparation for 1976 — which was going to be the big year."

TAPERING — the Dave Haller philosophy

To get a swimmer on the block ready to give that final big effort on the right day he (or she) must have:

RESTED, to allow the muscles and bodily systems to recover from the efforts of heavy training . . .

RELAXED, to relieve mental tensions . . .

REHEARSED, so that every technical detail of the race has been practised, plotted and prepared as an exercise of concentration.

These three Rs, in fact, make up "THE TAPER", the modern final preparation procedure involving drastic reductions in the training work-load. It is a balance between keeping the swimmer in condition, yet fully rested to produce an optimum performance when it matters.

A taper is a very individual thing and the amount of time it takes varies widely from swimmer to swimmer according to how much or how little work has been done in the months leading up to the event. And the planning towards the peak must not be a day too late, or a day too soon. It has got to be absolutely spot on.

10

1976

MONTREAL

Working up to the big one

The four years between Munich and Montreal were successful, exciting, happy and sometimes traumatic ones for Wilkie. And although he did not believe he could prepare mentally or physically for a target four years ahead, the year 1976 always had a particular significance, was something special. It could be said that it was the only year in which he set about fulfilling his true potential with absolute concentrated attention and, that overworked word, dedication.

"In the previous three years I had been thinking about my swimming and hoping to do well. But the Olympics, which had been at the back of my mind since I won my silver in Munich, was what I was really at and now I was so close to Montreal there was no fooling around.

"I really was careful. If I went to Cape Florida for a bit of snorkling I made sure I had my knife with me. It was a precaution I thought I should take. In a car, I drove a bit slower than usual. If I went out for a beer, I probably had one less than my normal quota. Little things like that, but they all built up.

"In the back of my mind in everything I did I was saying 'Take care of yourself David.' I rested more, ate better, took care of my health. If I felt sick at all I went to the health centre straight away. Before, if I had a cold or something, I just let it get better."

The swimming build-up started in late 1975, just after the Scot had been voted "Sportsman of the Year" by the Sports Writers' Association of Great Britain. The Miami University swim squad went to Cali, Colombia, the scene of David's World championships double triumph that summer, for a two-week training camp in preparation for the college winter season.

It was work, work, work, 12,000 metres a day, six days a week, with the focus on stroke technique. Wilkie and his coach Charlie Hodgson did a lot of talking and planning about 1976 and the conclusion was that if David could start well and maintain that through the year it would be a good omen for Montreal.

This talk was important because Wilkie usually started the year slowly. But not this time. Back in Miami, there were a few college meetings and David found he was swimming better than he had ever done before.

"I really knew this was going to be a good year. If I could keep myself out of trouble, in good condition all the time, there was nothing to stop me doing very well in Montreal.

"The coaches in Miami (Charlie Hodgson and head coach Bill Diaz) put a lot of confidence in me. They kept saying 'you are the best breaststroke swimmer in the world . . . there is no one who is going to beat you . . . there's no way you can lose the 200 metres.' And they had me believing it."

It was not only Wilkie and the coaches who thought that way. David's swimming performances made his Miami squad-mates, including his British Olympic team racing partner Paul Naisby, become believers. In the past, in training, David was not too bothered if others sometimes led the way. Not in 1976. He was going his best all the time, trying to beat them by as much as possible.

"I really pushed into my own mind that if someone was six seconds slower than me racing then he was going to be six seconds slower than me in training too. And this approach made me train much harder than ever before."

Even with his studies, Wilkie was managing to cover 10,000 yards a day in two sessions, plus muscle-building pulley and strength work. An important part of his preparations were the remedial exercises for a chronic back condition, prescribed by Tony Power, the British team physiotherapist.

Wilkie had been bothered since 1973 with a slipping vertebra in his upper back which at times affected his training. He saw two orthopaedic specialists who treated him whenever it went out, but the Power programme of preventative exercises, which David carried out religiously, were most beneficial of all. And he was also careful about lifting anything heavy.

"I did the exercises for at least 30 minutes every day. I used to get down to the pool early in the afternoons and get a bit of a sun-tan at the same time. And when Tony saw me in Montreal he said, as far as he was concerned, there was nothing wrong."

That Power was in Montreal at all and able to work with the British team, took a lot of undercover organising. He wasn't one of the official Olympic squad physios and the security at the pool was every bit as tight as the reports indicated. But the team wanted him and ways were found, back-doors opened, for him to be there and play his part in Wilkie's great moment.

January to March was taken up with inter-college matches, with David swimming the 200 yards breaststroke and 200 yards medley and the breaststroke leg in the medley relay, leading up to the National Collegiate Athletics Association championships, the world's greatest short-course meeting, from March 25th to 27th.

The Miami squad tapered off their training, and shaved down for the championships at Brown University, Providence, Rhode Island, where the shallowness of the 25-yard pool made for slow times and produced only a few new American records.

Wilkie did not swim as well as he had hoped, but still defeated his rival John Hencken by a second in the 200 yards breaststroke in a United States open record of 2 min. 00.73 sec. and came second to Hencken in the 100 yards breaststroke and to Lee Engstrand in the 200 yards medley, beaten each time by narrow margins.

Five days later, after an East to West-coast flight, a three-hour time change, and a switch from short course to long course racing, the Miami mob turned out in the Amateur Athletic Union national championships of the United States. Traditionally this A.A.U. spring meeting is also swum short course but in 1976, because of the early July date for the Olympics, the event was held in a 50-metre pool in Long Beach, California.

With so much energy expended in the tense inter-collegiate rivalry at the N.C.A.A. meeting, this new challenge was something of an anti-climax for swimmers more ready for rest than racing. And the thought of holding their tapers for another week and living out of suitcases at yet another motel seemed all too much. In fact, Wilkie

The Christchurch scoreboard tells the medley story. Jungle Boy and the Water-Baby . . . David with Australia's Jenny Turrall, 13 years old, winner of the 400 metres freestyle at the Commonwealth Games of 1974.

Merry moments in Vienna. Dave Haller, the British team coach, hamming it up as he tel
new European champion Wilkie how breaststroke should be swum . . . and pays th
penalty as he gets pulled by a track-suited David Leigh and pushed by David Wilkie an
company into the training pool.

confessed that he didn't really want to go. But the coaches wanted it and so he did.

"I was tired of swimming and when I got there, even though I was only doing 4,000 m. a day, I was swimming very badly. I couldn't even break 33 sec. for 50 metres and I'm usually 30-point something. But all of us, including John Hencken, were in the same boat. I had thought it would be a psychological advantage if I could beat John and, once I got there, it became important for me to win. Yet if I had thought it was an important meet earlier I might have done better . . . even broken the world records."

In the event Wilkie surprised himself. The closer he got to his races, the better he was swimming and he finished the four days of high quality racing as the only competitor, man or woman, to win three titles. He beat Hencken in the 100 metres breaststroke by 23 hundredths of a second in 1 min. 6.46 sec. He beat Hencken again over 200 metres, this time by more than three seconds, and his 2 min. 18.48 sec. was only 27 hundredths outside the American's world record. Wilkie's hat-trick gold came in the 200 metres medley in which he set European and Commonwealth figures of 2 min. 6.25 sec., the second fastest performance of all time and only 17 hundredths outside the world record held by Bruce Furniss, of the United States.

It was the first time Wilkie had won an A.A.U. title and here he was with three. And he had missed annexing three world records by a total aggregate of seven tenths of a second.

"To beat John twice was really great. It did a lot for me psychologically and after beating him in the 100, which isn't really my race, I knew I could do it again. These victories helped during the summer training. You get a bit down and tired of it all and then you remember you won three races at Long Beach and that lifts you."

At last David got his long awaited rest — two weeks away from the pool, apart from a daily 1,000 yards stretch-out paddle. It gave him time for some fishing trips down at the Florida Keys where — shades of Ceylon — he never caught much, but was able to relax and forget about everything.

With examinations out of the way in early May, Montreal started to loom larger and it was conference time with Charlie Hodgson again, setting up a new schedule for the two months before the Games. For the first of these it was 12,000 metres a day, long-course work in the morning aimed at endurance and short-course concentration on stroke and sprints in the afternoons.

"It was easy to get back into hard training. But what wasn't so easy was the fact that there were only about nine of the squad left — Paul Naisby, Sean Maher and myself working for the British team and five or six trying for the U.S. Olympic trials. It's not so easy to train with a small group . . . not much fun, not much competition in work-outs . . . and a bit depressing."

Yet in the first week back Wilkie was doing some remarkable times. He found he could kick (legs only) 200 metres breaststroke in 2 min. 50 sec. — ten seconds faster than before — and not just once, but about ten repetitions at a time with only short rests in between.

"The next week I suffered like the devil for training so hard and went down a bit. But I was so much into training that even when I was tired I was pushing everything I did. That was something I had never done before. I used to lay off a bit when I got tired. By sweating through I got onto a new plateau, a new level for both training and racing. Repeating the times over and over again I got very, very fit and the rest of the summer was used to maintain that fitness."

Wilkie wasn't afraid of reaching his peak too soon because he was working so hard. At the same time, he didn't enter any competitions. Seven weeks before his first race in Montreal he started his taper. For the first two of these, the daily training distance dropped to 10,000 metres, then came two weeks on 8,000 metres. By the time he joined the British squad in Montreal and team coach Dave Haller took charge, there were three weeks of taper left. Now David went down to 7,000 metres, in two sessions, and in the last days was not doing more than 3,000 metres a day.

The British squad officials were absolutely delighted with Wilkie's condition. Coach Haller looked at his swimming form and was happy with what he saw. Doc. McIntyre, who had known David since he was a 13-year-old, said he had never seen him in such superb physical shape. And the phlegmatic physio Power was almost ecstatic over Wilkie's fitness.

So there it was, everything going well: taper, training, body and mind. As David put it: "Everything was coming up roses." There was only one thorny problem — the cramped living conditions in the crowded Olympic village — and that was outside the control of Wilkie's back-up team, outside the control even of the British Olympic Association, though they did all that was possible to alleviate things.

Strangely the tight security did not bother David at all. With memories of Munich and the Israeli murders, he knew the security had to be strict and he accepted this. What came hard was sharing a three-roomed apartment with 11 other people, with only one bathroom and toilet. It meant disturbed nights especially, which could have been the kiss of death to his medal hopes.

"I was in with Gordon Hewit, Alan McClatchey, Gordon Downie, John Mills and Kevin Burns. It was a good room and everyone in it wanted to swim well, not just compete. The first week there was, inevitably, a lot of talking about what we had been doing all summer and we weren't getting to sleep until midnight, two hours later than we would have liked.

"Even when we had settled down, with people coming in at different times at night, using the toilet and switching on the lights, it was difficult. And when you are in the mood when anything and everything disturbs you, once you are awake you have a hard time getting back to sleep again.

"Your mind is working all the time, regurgitating facts and there was a lot to think about, a lot going on and I found it very hard. Of course, I was excited, too, so even at night-time the adrenaline was still flowing and with so much pent-up nervous energy my mind was too active for sleep. Even after my races I was still sleeping very badly. This is unusual for me. I enjoy my sleep and get a lot of it. I did rest in the afternoons, but it put me off a bit."

It was the first time in Wilkie's seven years in big-time competition that he had experienced this kind of pre-event excitement. The feeling began two weeks before his first Montreal races and got him to the stage where he was lying in bed, turning fitfully, thinking "Oh, God! I wish I could go to sleep."

11

1976

MONTREAL

Britain's first medal   but 'only' a silver

O ften since Montreal, and even at times while the Games were still on, the question has been asked whether David would have won both breaststroke events had they come the other way round in the programme . . . if the 200 metres had come before the 100 metres.

Many thought if Wilkie had got the 200 metres out of the way first — and won — the euphoria would have given him an unbeatable advantage to take into the shorter event. He wouldn't have had to worry about his arch rival John Hencken, there would not have been any comparable tension, there would have been everything to gain and nothing to lose. David didn't, and still doesn't, see it that way.

"Yes, I accept it could have been to my advantage, but also it could have worked the other way. I could have gone into the 200 metres without knowing what I was capable of doing. I knew I had the endurance for the longer race . . . what I didn't know was how fast I could go at the beginning. So the 100 metres was a good stepping-stone and very valuable to my 200 metres.

"Also, if the 200 metres had come first and I had beaten Hencken, this might have fired him up so much, made him so mad, he might have swum even faster in the 100 metres than he did in fact. Basically, the Olympic programme suited me the way it was, because I like to have my most important race later when I know exactly what everything is about."

History has already recorded the fact that Wilkie took the silver medal — Britain's first of any sport at the Montreal Games — behind Hencken in the 100 metres having raced a heat and semi-final on Monday, July 19th, and a tense final on Tuesday, the 20th.

Hencken, the favourite, set world record figures in each round. He equalled his two-year-old mark with a 1 min. 3.88 sec. in a heat and cut this to 1:3.62 in finishing three-tenths ahead of Canada's Graham Smith in the second semi-final. He reduced these figures still further, to 1:3.11 in beating Wilkie by 0.32 in the final. It was a magnificent stint of superb sprinting. Indeed, Hencken was the only competitor to set world marks in all three rounds of any event at the Games. And Wilkie's European and Commonwealth record of 1:3.43 in second place was nearly a second faster than he had done before and 0.45 inside Hencken's pre-Games world mark.

With only one major 100 metres victory in his career to his credit — that over Hencken at the A.A.U. championships in Long Beach the previous April — David knew he had a hard task even before he had swum a single stroke in the Olympics. And for better or worse he decided on a course of action, in an attempt to fool his rivals, which alarmed his supporters. It was something that David did not even discuss with coach Haller . . . something he alone decided. This was to try to kid people that he wasn't a serious medal contender in this sprint event. Whether he succeeded — or whether he only fooled himself — is now only a matter of academic conjecture.

"I made up my mind I was going to take the heat, semi-final and final as three different steps. In the heat, I decided I wouldn't shave down, or try 100 per cent. In the semi-final I didn't shave down completely and I did a couple of things that would put me off. I didn't talk to Dave Haller about this . . . he wouldn't have wanted me to do it . . . he doesn't like that kind of thing. And I didn't do it to amuse anybody either. It was gamesmanship . . . not psyching the others out, but faking them out . . . into believing I wasn't on form. It's something I learned in the States.

"So, seeing me in the heat, I hoped people would say 'Wilkie won't do anything'. And that's what they did say. In the semi-final I swam a little bit better, yet nowhere near what I knew I could do, to encourage people to think 'he won't be any danger in the final'. But I knew exactly what I was doing, otherwise I wouldn't have done it. Dave and I had worked out and Charlie Hodgson had told me as well, just what we thought would be needed to get through to the final."

Mathematically, the calculations were all right, but David still got a bit of a surprise in Heat Three. His fool-em tactic here was to adopt an old-fashioned, arm-swinging starting dive instead of the usual modern grab start technique. In this swimmers bend down to hold the starting block with both hands, then using their full body weight for propulsion, get a far faster, longer entry into the water. This ploy lost the Scot distance on the first lap, but, even so, he was shocked to find himself having to chase Canada's Smith to the first-place touch. In the end the men were given a dead-heat in 1 min. 5.19 sec. which was a second outside Wilkie's best time and a fractional improvement for Smith.

The V.I.P. at the pool that morning was Her Majesty The Queen, who had seen Britain's Duncan Goodhew and David Leigh, the Commonwealth champion, win their respective heats before Wilkie's battle with Smith. And they all made a right royal progress into the last 16.

There were two false starts to the first semi-final, each by the defending champion Nobutaka Taguchi of Japan, who surprisingly did not get through to the final. Wilkie, apparently unruffled, paced his race after a deliberately slow first length, from which he turned in fifth place, to touch just ahead of Italy's Giorgio Lalle in 1:04.29, only six hundredths of a second outside his European and Commonwealth records. Goodhew, with his fastest-ever 1:04.59, was third and qualified for the final.

But once again Wilkie got a shock and again Smith provided it. In the second semi-final, the young Canadian, 18 years old, set new Commonwealth figures of 1:03.92 as he chased world record-breaker Hencken home. Commonwealth champion Leigh finished seventh (1:05.91) and was eliminated.

Wilkie confessed he was a bit taken aback. "I knew Graham was a good competitor, but after his swim in the semi-final I thought 'My goodness it's going to be a good final.'" And so it was. Hencken, the only swimmer to go under 30 seconds for the first 50 metres (29.48), led from start to finish. At half distance David (30.45) was marginally sixth behind Lalle, Smith, Russia's Arvidas Iuozaytis and West Germany's Walter Kusch, with only 58 hundredths of a second (less than a metre) covering the men from second to eighth. Although Wilkie swam the second 50 metres 65 hundredths of a second faster than Hencken it was not enough to compensate for his one second leeway at the turn.

Hencken improved his semi-final world record time by another 0.51 of a second to beat Wilkie by half a second with 1 min. 3.11 sec.

David's European and Commonwealth record of 1 min. 3.43 sec., nearly a second faster than he had ever done before, was precisely the time he thought he could do . . . that he believed could win. And Russia's little-known Iuozaytis, who incidentally speaks excellent English, came through in an outside lane (No. 1) to snatch the bronze from Canada's Smith.

"Looking back I think I could have won that final. My dive was OK, but when I kicked into my stroke my legs kicked air . . . I must have gone too deep in my dive. This cost me easily three-tenths of a second, practically the difference between coming first or second. I don't know why it happened, maybe it was because I was so eager to get going and, in my eagerness, was in too much of a hurry.

"Of course if I'd been in the lane next to Hencken and been able to see him, I probably wouldn't have let myself be so far behind on the first length. And if my dive had gone right . . . who knows? It is easy to say all these things in hindsight. I thought it would take a 1 min. 3.4-ish to win and I did that. But John did better . . . a damn good time."

Hencken was in lane 4, normal practice in swimming for the fastest qualifier, with the next two fastest, Smith and Kusch, on either side of him in lanes 5 and 3. Wilkie, one hundredth of a second slower than the West German, had to settle for lane 6, still good, but not one to give him contact with Hencken, the only man who mattered to him in the race.

Maybe David's gamesmanship in the semi-final, which lost him that important position beside his great rival in the final, cost him more than he gained by the subterfuge. Wilkie went into the 100 metres hoping for victory and he was disappointed afterwards, for a little while, even though he won the silver medal. But he was nothing like as disappointed as he would have been had it been the 200 metres final that night. And that story is still to be told . . .

12

1976

MONTREAL

A calculated risk

Wilkie could not do very much in the way of celebrating his 100 metres breaststroke silver — Britain's first medal of the Montreal Games. As an immediate thing, there was the 4 x 100 metres medley relay, with an outside chance of the bronze medal, but in the background the giant, the 200 metres breaststroke, was looming.

Of course, British team-mates and officials made a fuss of David and telegrams from relations and friends arrived at the Olympic village. But, basically, it was swimming business as usual, with the relay on Thursday, July 22nd, next on David's agenda.

Picking the British squad involved coach Haller and team manager Alan Clarkson from York in a lot of heart-searching. Only one place in the four-man team was definite . . . Wilkie on breaststroke in the final, for in swimming, unlike athletics, the same competitors do not have to take part in heat and final of a relay. And Britain had any number of permutations for the first, third and fourth legs of backstroke, butterfly and freestyle respectively.

The snag was that neither Scotland's Jimmy Carter nor Gary Abraham from Southampton had ever done a sub-minute 100 metres backstroke, whereas most of the other medal-challenging nations were counting on 57 seconds or better and with America hoping for something under 56 seconds.

On top of which the two Britons, Abraham 5 ft. 9 in. (1.75 m.) and Carter 5 ft. 10 in. (1.77 m.), were not the tallest fellows in the world. Not small, but not big up against America's John Naber 6 ft. 6 in. (1.98 m.), Canada's Steve Pickell 6 ft. 4½ in. (1.94 m.), or West Germany's Klaus Steinbach 6 ft. 3½ in. (1.91 m.). And size and reach are important in relays. That was the first problem.

The second was what to do about team captain Brian Brinkley, who had opted out of swimming in either the 100 metres butterfly or freestyle in the Games but, on past performances, was still potentially the fastest man for either leg.

Where was this great competitor to be used to the best advantage? Should he be on butterfly in preference to City of London policeman John Mills, who, two days earlier, had just missed the final of the individual 100 metres butterfly having broken Brinkley's British record in a heat, and call up the giant American-Scot, 6 ft. 5 in. (1.95 m.) Gordon Downie, for freestyle?

Or would it aggregate better for the team to have Mills on butterfly and leave Brinkley in his favourite relay position as the freestyle anchor man, ready to lift the team on his broad shoulders? Brian, the British 100 metres freestyle record-holder, had done it in the 4 x 200 metres relay the night before when he turned a 3½ second deficit into a 0.15 sec. bronze medal victory over West Germany.

Brinkley was involved more than that for in their backstroke dilemma Haller and Clarkson had even contemplated putting the big Bedford man in first. Their thinking was that Brinkley was a good all-round swimmer — he won silver medals for the 200 and 400 metres individual medley at the 1974 Commonwealth Games — even though he was untried in an individual backstroke race at this level. And he was 6 ft. 3 in. (1.90 m.)!

So for the morning heat, it came down to mathematics and who they could afford to use, who dare they leave out and be sure of qualifying — and who was going to do what.

The answer came out — Abraham on backstroke and he was promised that a sub-minute time would guarantee him this berth in the final. Duncan Goodhew, the North Carolina State University student from Sussex, who had been seventh in the 100 metres breaststroke final, as David's stand-in. Mills on butterfly and Kevin Burns, from Sheffield, on freestyle. Wilkie and Brinkley were rested for the final and Carter also was packed off to bed in case he was needed for the backstroke . . . provided, of course, the second team got Britain through to the evening final.

It was a bold, bold, gamble and it paid. The squad qualified as the fourth fastest, cutting 0.45 sec. from the British record in the process with 3 min. 52.35 sec., though not before a few heart-stopping moments when there was an ominous blank on the score-board where

Britain's time and placing should have been. Had the squad been disqualified? No! the electronic timing had gone on the blink.

As a matter of record, the Americans, with a reserve team, broke the world record with 3:47.28, Canada, with one reserve, set Commonwealth figures of 3:50.61 and West Germany, with two substitutes, equalled their own European record, to the hundredth of a second, with 3:51.57.

Yet the heat swim did not solve Britain's backstroke problem. Though Abraham's 60.24 sec. was better than anything Carter had done, he still had not broken the minute barrier. However, in the end, it was decided that the final line-up would be Carter, Wilkie, Mills and Brinkley.

The race went better for Britain than expected, but America, Canada and West Germany swam more superbly. Carter excelled himself with his first under-the-minute time of 59.60, a British record. But Naber with 55.89, Pickell 57.58 and Steinbach 57.82 had already got their squads into medal-winning positions while, at the Carter to Wilkie take-over, Britain were back in sixth place.

David had his best-ever breaststroke split time (1 min. 2.81 sec.) to get Britain up to fourth and close one second of the gap behind West Germany. But Hencken (1:2.50) and Smith (1:2.59), swimming as men inspired, edged further ahead in first and second places.

Mills put up his best butterfly time to stay fourth and Brinkley held off a great freestyle challenge from Russia's Andrey Krylov — whose 50.20 sec. on this leg was bettered only by America's Jim Montgomery (49.57) — to stay there.

The American first team of Naber, Hencken and Matt Vogel, who had already won the Olympic individual titles for their speciality strokes, and Montgomery, who was to take the freestyle sprint crown in a world record 49.99 on the last day, aggregated 3:42.22 to trim 5.06 sec. off the world figures set by their second team in the heats. Canada (3:45.94) and West Germany (3:47.29) also cut back on the Commonwealth and European marks they had set respectively in the morning. Britain (3:49.56) and the other four finalists finished in national record times.

"I found it a hard race to get ready for. We knew we were going to be way, way down after the backstroke and it was going to be up to me to make up as much of the lost ground as possible. I knew we had a chance of the bronze medal and I was going to swim my best for the team. But when you dive in so far behind it is a bit of a disappointment, even if you are expecting it.

"Jimmy swam very very well and being realistic I don't think we could have expected any more than we did. But it was still hard diving in where I did and, of course, it was the same for the rest of the guys coming in after me. It was my fastest time but other than that, well . . .! I swim to win — and it was impossible to win that one. The Americans had just about got it before the race started."

Nothing, bar disqualification, could have prevented the United States victory. Carter would have had to break the world 100 metres backstroke record of 55.49 sec. for Britain to have beaten Canada for the silvers and improve his pre-Games time by three seconds even to defeat West Germany for the bronzes.

13

1976

MONTREAL

The golden day

David's golden day, July 24th, 1976, started just after 6 a.m. when he was woken by Dougie McIntyre, the British team's regular doctor who because of restrictive rules had to be fiddled on to the Olympic squad as assistant team manager. Then it was breakfast, a very small one — some instant food, raisin bread and butter, washed down with a glass of milk — because Wilkie doesn't like to eat too much before racing.

He was down at the pool by 8.30, went through his exercise sequence, had a 25-minute warm-up, checking his stroke, doing a couple of sprints, and satisfied himself that he was swimming well and easily. Then came a massage from Tony Power and the anxious waiting for the start.

"I was more nervous for that 200 metres heat in Montreal than for any other competition in all my life. I was in the last one of the four and I sat with Dave Haller during the others and I wanted to know everything . . . everybody's times, their splits, even what they had done for the first 12½ metres. It was silly really, asking for all kinds of useless information, because I didn't need to know these things. I suppose I was filling my mind up with something, probably covering up my nervousness.

"In fact, I had thought about the race already and knew exactly what I was going to do . . . the time I was aiming for. But the times of the early heats were surprisingly slow and I thought to myself 'I hope I don't go that slow.'"

David was looking upon his heat as an experiment, aiming for a 2 min. 19 sec.-something. The idea was to go out hard for the first

100 metres to see if it hurt, then ease up on the third and fourth lengths. And that is the way it went.

"The first 100 metres came very nicely (1 min. 6.88 sec.), my stroke was good and on the last two lengths I held back. It didn't hurt much and I was surprised really that my 2:18.29 (an Olympic record, only eight hundredths outside John Hencken's world record and six hundredths outside Wilkie's European and Commonwealth figures) was so good."

The next fastest were the American trio, Rick Colella, who had won heat 2 in a short-lived Olympic mark of 2:21.08, Hencken, who won heat 3 in 2:21.23 and Charlie Keating, second in Wilkie's heat in 2:22.22.

They must have been shattered as the Briton's time went up . . . three seconds in hand over the field of 29. And a little bit of gamesmanship on the bath-side by Wilkie and Haller did nothing for the morale of the United States team, who were looking for a clean sweep of the 13 men's swimming titles having already won nine in succession.

As our hero explained: "After the heats, Dave Haller and I walked past American coach Don Gambril and Dave shouted out so that Don could hear, 'well, David, a 2:15 tonight then!' Yes, it was a laugh in a way, but we weren't joking, we were serious." It was even more serious than Haller knew.

"Whatever I do in morning heats, I know I am going to swim better at night. And during the 200 metres heats I thought I could drop three seconds in the final. I didn't tell anybody and I don't think that even Dave thought I could, despite what he said for Gambril's benefit. I believe Dave was thinking of 2:16 and I didn't tell him I wanted to do 2:15."

Even though Colella had the second best heat time, the only man who came into the Wilkie pre-final reckoning was defending champion Hencken, the arch rival, the man who had beaten the Scot into the silver medal spot in Munich four years before. Yet Hencken was dismissed almost arrogantly by Wilkie in four sentences.

"John was three seconds behind me and I knew for him to beat me on the night he'd have to drop six seconds on his time. So, logically, I knew after the heats there was no way he could win. I thought nobody else in the final would do much better than 2:20.

Really, I knew the race was as good as won so long as something didn't go wrong."

But the knowledge did not bring relaxation, though it did bring, for the first time in Montreal, a sort of calmness born of confidence. Wilkie went to bed in the afternoon, read a little, napped a little, listened to jazz music a little, yet calm though he might have felt the gold medal excitement was building up.

"There was an overspill of energy jumping around inside me and my body couldn't reach any state of complete rest. But even though my body was still going up and down after the heats, my mind became calm.

"I was ready for the final and I was excited about it, but it was all positive thinking. There were no negative thoughts, like coming second or third . . . only about winning."

Physio Tony Power can confirm just how calm David was before the final. "We had a pre-race routine, so that the swimmers could know exactly how things would go and didn't have to worry. And on that day I shall never forget, David and I went through our regular 20-minute programme of massage and stretching exercises. I timed this to finish about 15 minutes before he had to report for his final, to give him time to talk to Dave Haller and get everything ready for his race.

"David was the coolest person I have ever seen. And when I had finished my part of his preparations, he said, 'Well, you'd better go upstairs now and watch.' That was all he said, but I could almost hear the unspoken end of what he didn't say . . . 'go upstairs now and watch me WIN!' "

A little before eight o'clock on that Saturday night the stage was set for gold and glory. As the loudspeakers blared the Olympic entry music, "March of the Athletes", the eight gladiators were led to the start, with Wilkie in the middle of the bunch as the fastest qualifier. As usual, he was muffled up in a hooded towelling robe, over track suit, tee shirts and trunks, with the whole outfit topped as always by a tartan cap. This was a new one which Dougie McIntyre had brought from Scotland especially for Montreal and he gave it to David before the swimming started.

Wilkie saw Union Jacks fluttering in the predominantly American and Canadian crowd and waved towards them, hoping that somewhere among those British contingents his parents would be sitting. But his thoughts were all about the final and what it meant to him... about starting it, swimming it, about winning it and how it was going to be. It was all in his mind, calm and clear and concentrated, in spite of the shouts and cheers from the packed crowd, the peering television cameras and the hovering officials.

"I had talked about the race before with Dave and he told me what he thought I should do — be with Hencken for the first 100 and then let go for the second half, turn it on, really go. So as we went round the bath-side I was running over that in my mind, drilling myself how I was going to do it.

"And I was thinking as well about the best moment to take my little warm-up swim in the diving pool behind me . . . whether I would wait until my name had been announced, or go in before."

The men lined up, from lane 1 (on the right-hand side of the pool facing the course) like this:

1. *Nikolay Pankin, of the Soviet Union. Olympic 100 metres bronze medallist in 1968, European 100 metres champion in 1970 and 1974 and runner-up to Wilkie in the 200 metres in 1974. Age 27. Heat time 2 min. 22.82 sec.*
2. *Graham Smith from Canada. Seventh in the 1975 World championships. Age 18. Heat time 2 min. 22.24 sec.*
3. *John Hencken, of the United States, who beat Wilkie into second place in the 200 metres at the 1972 Munich Games, winner of the 100 metres title in Montreal four days earlier, the world record holder for 100 and 200 metres breaststroke (1:3.11 and 2:18.21). Age 22 (seven weeks younger than Wilkie). Heat time 2 min. 21.23 sec.*
4. *David Wilkie, of Great Britain. Olympic 200 metres silver medallist 1972 and 100 metres runner-up in Montreal. World 100 metres champion 1975 and 200 metres champion in 1973 and 1975, European and Commonwealth 200 metres champion and 100 and 200 metres record holder (1:3.43 and 2:18.23). Age 22. Heat time 2 min. 18.29 sec.*
5. *Rick Colella, U.S.A. Pan-American 200 metres champion 1971 and 1973, fourth in Munich and runner-up to Wilkie in the 1975 World 200 metres championship. Age 24. Heat time 2 min. 21.08 sec.*

6. *Charlie Keating, America's No. 3. Age 20. Heat time 2 min. 22.22 sec.*
7. *Arvidas Iouzaytis, of the Soviet Union. 100 metres bronze medallist in Montreal. Age 20. Heat time 2 min. 22.59 sec.*
8. *Walter Kusch, of West Germany, who advanced into this final through the disqualification of Wilkie's Miami team-mate Paul Naisby, from Sunderland, for a minor technical turning infringment during the heats. Sixth in the 200 metres at the 1972 Munich Olympics, European 100 metres silver medallist and 200 metres bronze medal winner in 1974. Age 22. Heat time 2 min. 22.95 sec.*

Wilkie took his loosening-up dip while Pankin, Smith and Hencken were being announced. And Hencken also snatched a brief plunge in the diving pool, though he studiously avoided Wilkie in the process.

Not that David noticed particularly. He wasn't thinking about anything except his personal problems and certainly Hencken was not among them.

"There were more important things in hand than thinking about who you were swimming against. You have to worry about yourself, and how you really are. I felt good and I made sure I didn't get cold after my dip by wrapping a towel around me. And then I adjusted my goggles."

Those goggles, like his cap, very much an unmistakable Wilkie trade-mark, play an important part in the Scot's competitive equipment. As well as helping him to get clearer vision above and below the water during races, they provide the final diversion for his mind before the start.

"My goggles, you know, take a lot of my anxiety away. By worrying about the damn things and whether they are going to fall off (they never have!) I keep my mind occupied before the gun. It has always been part of my make-up on the block and I find it good to have something to do with my hands."

David may find his goggle-fiddling soothing. But his last-minute twitching and touching inspires quite the opposite feeling on those of us watching, even on those who know him well. And never was this more so than on that tensely dramatic night in Montreal.

Wilkie has a vague recollection that there was one false start but

n-up pose. David in Vienna (1974) with his two European championships gold medals,
the 200 metres breaststroke and medley.

Wilkie at play. Still competitive (above) with Montreal modern pentathlon gold medall Jim Fox, in a trial of strength (Photo: Daily Express) and canoeing in Christchurch, little relaxation away from the pool during the 1974 Commonwealth Games, w Dundee's Debbie Simpson (Photo: Bill Black).

*portsman of the Year'' for 1975. A whiskered Wilkie with the Sports Writers' Associ-
on of Great Britain trophy and the Tony Duffy souvenir picture of his World cham-
nships victory in Cali (Photo: Derek Rowe). And (above) Charlie Hodgson, one of
University of Miami coaches.*

The two Davids who had so many breaststroke battles for Britain and against each othe Wilkie and (right) Leigh, the Commonwealth champion and World and European bronz medallist.

isn't sure. In fact, Colella followed by Hencken went in before the gun — which had B.B.C. swimming expert Hammy Bland, a former British team coach, theorising about an attempt to put Wilkie off.

"If there was a false start, it didn't affect me. And even if there had been a delay and we'd had to wait even half an hour, it might have affected me a bit, but it wouldn't have made any difference."

This sounds somewhat boastful, which is not Wilkie's intention, nor is it in his character. Rather it is an honest reaction to a sincere and confident belief.

Finally the eight men got away to a good start and it soon became clear that it was to be a two-swimmer race with only one likely to be there at the end. It went exactly as planned, with Wilkie ahead of Hencken at 50 metres which was a bit of a surprise. The Scot remembered what Haller had said and slowed down, lengthened his stroke, and just swam with the American, though a little behind, until the end of the second length.

Hencken turned in 1 min. 6.09 sec. to Wilkie's 1:06.49 with Smith and Colella one second behind the American and Briton respectively. As Wilkie came out of that half-distance turn he said to himself: "This is it" and really pushed from then on.

"On the third length I moved and I thought John might come with me, but he didn't seem to have anything. And even though he wasn't that much behind at the last turn (Hencken actually was 0.66 sec. or just under a metre down) I knew that was it . . . that he couldn't bring it back on the fourth length.

"I stopped even being aware of him for our contest was over and it just became a race against the clock and as good a time as possible."

Up the fourth length it was Wilkie the majestic, Wilkie the magnificent, Wilkie the breaststroke King. As David had known after the morning heat no one was going to beat him for the gold medal. And at the finish, as the racing commentators say: "No doubt about the winner."

So, there he was at the bath end, the first British man for 68 years to win an Olympic swimming title and wearing the World, European and Commonwealth crowns as well, with every dream fulfilled in his mind as well as in fact — except for one. And David waited for that climax to come.

While the 9,000 fans shouted and screamed, clapped and cheered, waved their flags and blew their whistles, as commentators talked and typewriters tapped, the white-capped Briton savoured the moment, still resolutely facing the end of the pool.

"I knew I'd won it, so I took my time before I turned round to see what time I had done. It felt like 10 seconds . . . it may have been anything, but it was on purpose. I wanted to capture the whole glory of the moment and finding out my time was going to be like the icing on the cake.

"It wasn't easy to wait. I wanted to turn round straight away and know. But I said to myself 'I'll wait' . . . you see, the time was the only thing I needed to know.

"And when I did look round and saw 2 min. 15.11 sec. on the scoreboard, I couldn't believe it. When you've broken the world record and your own best by more than three seconds, and in that kind of competition, it's a great feeling.

"It's something you dream about doing, but when you do it it is so much different. You have proved to yourself that you are a good swimmer and that you have been capable of doing that all the way along.

"It was proof that the race had been swum well . . . proof that all the training had been right and worthwhile . . . proof to my coaches too that what they had been doing for me had also been right."

And not until that moment of total success did David react to his triumph raising his arms in glory above the water to acknowledge the plaudits from the fans to the Olympic champion.

So, the tables were turned. Hencken had to settle for the silver this time. He may not have been pleased about this, but he must have anticipated defeat. And he must have been pleased with his time of 2 min. 17.26 sec., a second faster than his old world record. Colella, third in 2:19.20, improved his best by two seconds. In fact, only Pankin of the eight finalists did not do better than ever before. The 200 metres breaststroke was the only men's title the Americans did not win — a fact that reflected tremendous credit on United States talent and training.

Whatever Wilkie felt, and his mind must have been like a kaleidoscope, there must have been one feeling of relief — that his dream of finishing second had not come true. Because that is what he did dream and on more than one occasion.

"It was terrible. I probably dreamed it more than twice, but I can only remember it twice. I don't usually remember my dreams, but I remember those.

"I didn't think it was a dream when I received my gold medal. I knew that was real and though I don't actually remember walking to the victory rostrum I was well aware of all that happened when I got there.

"Watching earlier medal ceremonies, I thought what an emotional moment it must be. And it was. Getting up there, listening to our National Anthem, seeing the Union Jack go up, with all the people there, my family and the British team and thinking of all the people at home, the millions watching on television, it was tremendously satisfying and gratifying for me.

"It was great, it really was . . . I was extremely proud. It was difficult to control my feelings, not to cry. And I really didn't want to control the way I felt and I wouldn't have been ashamed if I had cried."

In fact, as his eyes misted, his mouth twitched and his chin buckled, David was saved by the ending of "God Save The Queen".

"Suddenly it was all so much more real than I had imagined. You think about winning a gold medal. But when you actually do, you are living it. I was well aware of this. It was something I had been looking forward to . . . something I could understand and I loved it.

"On the rostrum it was my time, completely mine, it belonged to me and nobody else. But afterwards it belonged to a lot of other people. I remember walking round the pool with John and Rick, wondering how I should react to the applause.

"Most of all, I was wanting to hurry, to get round to the other side to see Dave Haller. I don't know why this was so important, but I just had to get to Dave and share the moment with him, because he was part of it. I wanted to see my parents and my Miami coach Charlie Hodgson as well . . . everyone there who had helped me achieve my success."

The one part of his golden day that Wilkie had not rehearsed over and over in his mind, was how he was going to react after his victory. And as he walked round the pool with his medal round his neck, the

Ceylon-born, Scottish-schooled, American-trained Briton suddenly discovered how very British he was. For it was the British fans, so heavily outnumbered by the American supporters, who got Wilkie's attention. His explanation was typical.

"I only waved at people who were waving British flags. A lot of people look on me as being very American and, perhaps, I was scared to take their acclaim, even though I shall be eternally grateful for all that Miami did for me.

"But I wanted to show the British supporters that I was swimming for Britain, that I was proud to be British and be part of the Great Britain team and I wanted to push this home to everyone."

FOUR YEARS APART

How the 1972 and 1976 Olympic 200 metres breaststroke titles were won
(positions in eight-men finals at each stage in brackets)

	DAVID WILKIE (GREAT BRITAIN)			JOHN HENCKEN (UNITED STATES)		
Distance	Total time	50 m split	100 m split	Total time	50 m split	100 m split
	m. sec.	sec.	m. sec.	m. sec.	sec.	m. sec.
Munich, 1972						
50 metres	33.45 (5)	33.45		31.55 (1)	31.55	
100 metres	1:11.37 (6)	37.92	1:11.37	1:08.34 (1)	36.79	1:08.34
150 metres	1:47.41 (3)	36.04		1:45.35 (1)	37.01	
200 metres	2:23.67 (2)	36.26	1:12.30	2:21.55 (1)	36.20	1:13.21
	European & Commonwealth record			World & Olympic record		
Montreal, 1976						
50 metres	31.24 (1)	31.24		31.32 (2)	31.32	
100 metres	1:06.49 (2)	35.25	1:06.49	1:06.09 (1)	34.77	1:06.09
150 metres	1:40.84 (1)	34.35		1:41.50 (2)	35.41	
200 metres	2:15.11 (1)	34.27	1:08.62	2:17.26 (2)	35.76	1:11.17
	World, Olympic, European & Commonwealth record					

14

1976

MONTREAL

. . . and the aftermath

Winning turned out to be more than just a gold medal and a few moments of glory in the pool. Wilkie had filled a hiatus in British sports history for it had been 68 years since one of his countrymen had claimed an Olympic swimming crown.

The last men winners were at the first London Games in 1908 at the White City where, in a 100 metres pool built in the centre of the athletics stadium, Henry Taylor from Chadderton, Lancashire, had won the 400 and 1,500 metres freestyle and a third gold in the 4 x 200 metres relay, while Frederick Holman became the first-ever 200 metres breaststroke champion.

Holman's winning time was 3 min. 9.2 sec. against David's 2 min. 15.11 sec., which in taking 3.10 sec. off the former world record has been computed as "the outstanding swimming performance of the Montreal Games". Had a magician waved a wand and put the two champions in the pool together, Holman would have been left trailing Wilkie by 57.18 metres at the finish.

Extending the event coincidence still further, the last Briton, man or woman, to win an Olympic swimming title was Anita Lonsbrough at the 1960 Rome Games in, as one might guess, the 200 metres breaststroke. And Anita was in Montreal, commenting on David's victory for B.B.C. radio.

From the moment David touched the bath end and became Olympic champion everything changed. An old life was over and a new one had begun, though at the time he was scarcely given a moment to appreciate that it was happening.

Even in the familiar television, radio and press interviews there was a new urgency, new demand. There was confusion, and bubbling excitement, especially by the British sports writers and supporters and it was difficult not to be swept away on the emotional tide.

Yet Wilkie, the student of mass communications at the University of Miami kept his cool and his poise. He answered the endless and repetitive questions sensibly, courteously and fluently and through it all came his essential "niceness".

There was even drama behind the scenes as B.B.C. television transmitted the triumph to the waiting millions at home in Britain. Commentator Alan Weeks confessed:

> "We had tremendous technical problems that night. The sound circuit went down, some said a slip of a switch was sending the British commentary to Yugoslavia! So we had to work part by microphone and part by telephone. But that race news just had to get across and David's victory gave me my proudest moment in 25 years of television broadcasting."

David had seen his mother and father only once since they had been in Montreal. It had been decided there should be no distractions from his swimming task. So as soon as his pool commitments were over he set about finding them and this proved a little more difficult than winning his Olympic title.

> "I was supposed to meet my parents at the main entrance to the pool, but I couldn't find them. I was outside the door and they were waiting inside. So I had to leave a message while I went off to the B.B.C. studio and they met me there. We had planned a family get-together with my mother's cousin Muriel Strachan, who lives in Toronto, but it didn't work out like that . . . it all got rather public. So the family gathering, our private moment of being together, had to be put off until the following evening.
>
> "But there was champagne, although I don't think I drank very much. Then the messages began to roll in and I was amazed what a difference there was between winning an Olympic gold medal rather than a silver or a world title. The Olympics have that certain charisma. If you add together all the messages I received for my other victories and medals in the previous six years, they still wouldn't equal the telegrams and letters I received after winning in Montreal. It was nice, and good to think that people remembered me. I've kept them all and they are at home in Aberdeen."

There was a cable from the Prime Minister, signed just Jim Callaghan (that signature impressed David) and another from the

Minister for Sport, Denis Howell. Beverley Whitfield, the 1972 Olympic women's 200 metres breaststroke champion, wired and wrote from Australia. And Bobby McGregor, Scotland's last swimming medal winner (he took the 100 metres freestyle silver at the 1964 Games in Tokyo) cabled too. "Good old Bobby . . . he always sends me a telegram after each victory." There was a telex, from former world motor racing champion Jackie Stewart, another Scot, of course.

Messages came from Miami, from people Wilkie did and did not know. The letters of congratulations included three from his former boarding housemasters at Daniel Stewarts College in Edinburgh — Paul Maxwell, Dougie McMahon and Alan Fox. And to a man they said they had always known he had potential! He heard from swimmers and ex-swimmers . . . even from a rock band, playing in Paris, called Bad Company — though they certainly were not on this occasion.

"People have asked me if being a star is a burden and in a way it is, but it is something I am very happy to accept. When I went back to Aberdeen I was scared to go out of the house at one stage and when I stayed in the phone wouldn't stop ringing and people kept knocking at the door asking for autographs. Once when I went down town to a reception, they had to stop the traffic. At that time, the only way my mother and I could get away was to go out for a drive in the country.

"Now wherever I go people seem to recognise me, not so much as a person but as someone who has done something. It's as though they are showing their gratitude towards you, trying to be helpful and doing nice things for you . . . like being invited to go on the flight deck of a trans-Atlantic jet.

"I think an Olympic gold medal changes you from an ordinary person into a person people want to know. And they want to know what you are really like . . . is he different . . . how is he different?

"I don't think I have changed as a person even though my life certainly has changed. But give me a year or two and I am sure the changes in my life could bring about changes in my personality."

15

HENCKEN

We had nothing to say

How do you sum up four years in ten words? Even for a journalist that would be a challenge. David Wilkie achieved it without trying — which must be some sort of record. This is what he said: "John, it has been four good years . . . thanks a lot", and that was about the longest conversation he had ever had with his only real breaststroke rival in the world — John Hencken of the United States.

There have been many attempts to define the relationship between these two great champions, who had bestrode their specialist stroke like a twin Colossus, but by no means as twin souls. For sure they are not friends. Never have been. Never will be. But equally they are not enemies. Apparently they do not dislike each other. And although they have been extremely conscious of their own rivalry in the water, of their side-by-side confrontations, neither revenge, nor hatred, nor bitterness came into it, even though many suggestions along those lines have been made.

Those ten words were said by David to John while the two were still in the water after the Briton had beaten the American, the defending Olympic champion, in the 200 metres in Montreal. And really they say it all, for as far as Wilkie is concerned, it was the competition with Hencken that was important — not Hencken, the man. Yet that moment in Montreal must have been very strange for both of them.

Competitively, Wilkie won six of their 200 battles and all three of their long-course 200 metres clashes since 1973. Hencken's tally over the 100 was eight out of ten, losing only the N.C.A.A. short-course 100 yards race in 1974 and the A.A.U. long-course 100 metres battle of 1976.

Physically there is very little difference between them, though they look totally dissimilar. The Briton is 6 ft. 1 in. (1.86 m.) and 168 lb. (76 kg.); the American 5 ft. 11 in. (1.80 m.) and 170 lb. (77 kg.). Dark-haired David, broad shouldered and slim hipped, gives the impression of being longer and leaner. Fair-haired John, rounder-faced and pleasant looking, gives the impression of being stocky, though he is only two pounds the heavier. There is only 52 days difference in age with Hencken the younger.

Temperamentally it is hard to know who is different to whom, or whether there is any difference at all, though Wilkie thinks he is a warm fish and Hencken something of a cold one.

"The stories that John and I dislike each other don't have any background. You can't hate a person unless you know him and I really don't know John and he probably doesn't know me. We have never made a point of getting to know each other and I don't think we could hit if off as friends, even if we weren't swimming rivals. We are different kinds of people and have different interests. Certainly, in all honesty, he doesn't strike me as a man with whom I could have a close friendship.

"John appears to have cultivated areas of his nature that could assist him as a competitor and that has made him less warm in other areas . . . those involving personal and social contact with other people.

"I have cultivated the other side of my nature, too . . . the nasty competitive element. You have to have that. But really I am a sentimental person with my family and friends. If you consider me as a competitor and then as a human being, you will find a dual personality. But I am not a cold fish.

"We're friendly rivals, but there's not much communication between us. We say one or two words after the race . . . I don't think we've ever had a conversation that exceeded ten words. It's not because we hate each other. It's because we respect each other and we are rivals. We only have swimming in common . . . for me talking to John would be like talking to myself.

"I don't think we try to psych each other out at all, because we do have respect for each other and I think we know trying to do that wouldn't work.

"The relationship or lack of it wasn't done on purpose. It was just that way from the beginning. I didn't know who he was and he didn't know who I was at the 1972 Olympics in Munich (where

WILKIE versus HENCKEN
(1972-1976)

Event and Venue	100 Metres Breaststroke (* 100 yards)		200 Metres Breaststroke (* 200 yards)	
	Wilkie	**Hencken**	**Wilkie**	**Hencken**
Olympic Games, Munich	1:06.52 (8)	1:05.61 (3)	2:23.67 (2) *e/c*	2:21.55 (1) *w/o*
N.C.A.A., Knoxville s/c*	58.92 (4)	57.23 (1)	2:03.47 (1)	2:03.58 (3)
A.A.U. Cincinnati s/c*	58.81 (5)	57.44 (2)	2:05.71 (3)	2:03.94 (2)
World championships, Belgrade	1:05.74 (4)	1:04.02 (1) *w/wc*	2:19.28 (1) *w/wc/e/c*	2:19.95 (2)
N.C.A.A., Long Beach s/c*	56.72 (1)	56.94 (2)	2:03.40 (2)	2:01.74 (1) *us/n*
A.A.U., Dallas s/c*	56.58 (2)	55.50 (1)	2:01.84 (2)	Note No 1
N.C.A.A., Cleveland s/c*	56.30 (2)	55.59 (1)	Note No 2	2:00.83 (1) *us/n*
N.C.A.A. Providence s/c*	56.37 (2)	56.03 (1)	2.00.73 (1) *uso/n*	2:01.72 (2)
A.A.U., Long Beach	1:04.46 (1)	1:04.69 (2)	2:18.48 (1)	2:21.58 (2)
Olympic Games, Montreal	1:03.43 (2) *e/c*	1:03.11 (1) *w/o*	2:15.11 (1) *w/o/e/c*	2:17.26 (2)

Note No. 1   Hencken had the second fastest qualifying time (2:05.04) but scratched from the final due to illness.

Note No. 2   Wilkie had the second fastest time in the final (2:01.49) but was disqualified for using an illegal flutter kick on his fourth and fifth turns.

w/World record; *o*/Olympic record; *e*/European record;

c/Commonwealth record; *wc*/World championships record;

us/United States record; *uso*/United States open record;

n/N.C.A.A. record; *s/c*/short course (25 yards) pool.

Hencken beat Wilkie for the gold in the 200 metres) and we didn't even speak to each other. I suppose I was a little shy then — maybe John was shy, too. That Games was the first time we had met and I suppose our minds decided we weren't going to communicate with each other . . . not on purpose, but just the way it went. If you don't respond to a person the first time, you probably won't respond to them afterwards. Then, in 1972, I didn't dream that we would become such rivals in the next four years and I don't suppose John did either.

"Hencken wasn't a hero at any stage of my career and early on he wasn't a deadly rival either. It wasn't until I got involved in the American swimming scene that he did become a rival, a very close rival.

"Those four years in the States, I suppose, were four years of competition just with John Hencken. There were other people who were good at breaststroke, but they never threatened us at the serious meetings. Even Rick Colella (who was around throughout the Wilkie-Hencken years) never really did all that well against John and myself.

"John and I were always *in competition* at every meet — N.C.A.A., A.A.U. and the big ones. We were really the two people who had the monopoly. John did better in the 100 and I always thought he was the better sprint man. And I was better at 200 than he was . . . the result in Montreal showed that."

It did not take much push to get a bit of extra needle into the uneasy relationship. A quote in the programme at the 1974 N.C.A.A. championships at Long Beach, California, that . . . "only Batman and the Boy Wonder could beat Hencken in his favourite sprint event" set Wilkie off. After trailing in the early part of the 100 yards race, the Briton came through on the last 25 yards to beat Hencken by 0.22 sec. There were suggestions David should now be called the "Capped Crusader" but all he said after the race was: "They thought I could only swim the 200!" Then Hencken, sometimes called "The Rocket Man", brought Wilkie down to earth by winning the Scot's favourite 200 event!

A year later, after his 100 and 200 metres triumphs in the World championships — a meeting which Hencken decided to skip — Wilkie got very scratchy if people suggested that his Cali golds were tarnished because John had not been competing. "I enjoy racing more when he is there. And I hate it when people say 'if John had been there . . .'. Maybe if he had been in Cali I would have gone faster, beaten him and his world records."

The Hencken-Wilkie (or Wilkie-Hencken!) cold war stories flared again after the 100 metres in Montreal, where California's John from Culver City beat Scotland's Dave the Brave and they didn't shake hands. And at the press conference afterwards, with all the questions being shot at Hencken, the fed-up Wilkie finally, though quietly, walked out. Feud? Anger? Temper? Revenge? It wasn't any of those so far as David is concerned.

"I said in the dressing room, 'well you've won another gold John' and he said 'Yes'. But we didn't talk about the 200 metres. The atmosphere in there was a bit electric. We knew we had one more to go . . . that it wasn't over yet.

"It was the same old story . . . we didn't have anything to say to each other. There were a lot of things to be said, but we never did say them. This was a two-way thing. I can't criticise John for not talking to me, because I didn't talk to him.

"Not shaking hands wasn't done on purpose on my part. I am used to the winner making the first move, so I wasn't expecting to shake John's hand but for him to shake mine. Maybe it was done intentionally on his part . . . maybe it wasn't. But I wasn't going to shake his hand first because I'm used to it being done the other way round. He may have been trying to niggle me, but I wasn't trying to niggle him. But if I had won the 100 metres, I would have shaken his hand — not because I would have been happier at winning but because that's the etiquette as far as I am concerned.

"But the 200 was different and I won. I shook hands with John in the pool, on the victory rostrum too, and said: 'John, it has been four good years —thanks a lot.' He said, 'It certainly has.' I suppose that really summed it all up."

It did.

16

1970-1976

PLACES, PEOPLE AND PROBLEMS

Many remembered some best forgotten

David's amateur status was put at needless hazard in the winter of 1973, when an advertisement for goggles, which included a clearly identifiable picture of the Scot, though used *without* his permission, appeared in the March issue of the "Swimming Times", the official magazine of the Amateur Swimming Association.

It took many months, exchanges of letters between the International Olympic Committee, the International Amateur Swimming Federation (F.I.N.A.), the British Olympic Association, the A.S.A. and David himself, and caused a great deal of anxiety before Wilkie could be quite sure he would not be ruled out of competitive sport through no fault of his own.

The picture showed David in action, wearing his well-known cap with the Union Jack on the front . . . and goggles. Although his name was not mentioned, there was no doubt who it was and this was made doubly clear by the caption, which stated:

"The 1972 Olympic Games in Munich saw yet another progression in competitive swimming. A medal was won by a swimmer wearing Anti-Chlorine Goggles. We are proud to announce that these goggles were manufactured by . . ."

And David was the only British Olympic swimming medallist in Munich.

The F.I.N.A. international amateur rules at that time laid down, amongst other things, that an individual shall cease to be eligible to compete as an amateur:

"By *permitting* his name, his photograph or his performance in swimming to be used for advertising purposes."

The advertiser made every effort to ensure that Wilkie was not put at danger. He spoke to A.S.A. officials early in February and was led to believe it was all right to use the picture. And he confirmed his understanding of the conversation in writing two weeks before the advertisement appeared.

Not until after the advertisement had been published did he receive an answer to his letter and even then the A.S.A. spokesman wrote:

"As I read the present F.I.N.A. Amateur Law and the Regulations of the I.O.C. I cannot see how a swimmer could be penalised if a photograph of him wearing a manufactured product was used as an advertisement, provided he was unaware that this was to be done and that he did not obtain reward in any way whatsoever.

"However I have sent copies of this letter to the Authorities concerned asking for their ruling, in the meantime it would be advisable in the interests of the swimmer not to use a photograph for advertising purposes."

The "authorities" did not take the same complacent view. Dr. Harold Henning, the F.I.N.A. President, advised the A.S.A. that:

1. The advertiser should not be allowed to use the photograph of Wilkie wearing goggles in any advertising.
2. The I.O.C. Rule 26 as amended in November, 1971, debars those whose names or photographs have been used *at any time* with commercial advertising, from competing as amateurs.
3. The F.I.N.A. Rule 49 was quite clear.
4. The circumstances were quite similar to those relating to an incident in which another A.S.A. swimmer had become (unwittingly) involved in 1972.

The International Olympic Committee's Eligibility Commission, meeting in Lausanne, considered that there might have been a violation of their eligibility code and asked the British Olympic Association to investigate, which they did. Letters between the various people concerned were still being exchanged in June 1973.

Wilkie, out in Miami, was unaware that he had become involved in an amateur status wrangle until he was asked to write a letter stating that he had not given permission for his photograph to be used, nor had he received any payment in this respect. The first letter was not considered satisfactory and he had to write a second one, which was accepted.

"I was worried. I didn't know anything about it . . . I hadn't given my permission . . . I hadn't received any money. And I don't know how it could have been allowed to happen."

David was not alone in wondering that, but, fortunately, all was well in the end.

*   *   *

The Scot was the first big-time swimmer to wear goggles and a lot of people have followed him, particularly in Britain.

"The first pair I ever had were like big diving goggles, which were a great source of annoyance to my coach as I had to stop every length to let the water out. In 1971 I got a pair of proper swimming goggles and became very attached to them and have worn them — not the same pair of course — in training and all competitions since. The first major meet where I wore them was the 1972 Olympic trials for Munich.

"Eventually I became so used to them in training that I had to wear them in all my swimming. I don't think they are a great advantage, for my face is hardly in the water at all. But they do help me to see my turns and opponents better and I have become used to them and that is the important thing."

*   *   *

Along with his goggles and his cap, Wilkie's other very identifiable personal trade-mark is his moustache. He first tried to grow one in 1972, before the Olympics, but was not very successful at the time! It was not until he went to the University of Miami that he grew his first real one and he has had it ever since. The moustache does get trimmed for major races, but is never shaved off completely. Sometimes, in the rest season, David has also been seen with a goatee beard and more than luxuriant side-burns, but the shaggy look has to be sacrificed when swimming competition comes around and the manly growth is shaved off or severely pruned.

*   *   *

Wilkie's racing appearances in Britain were spasmodic. In the early days, holidays with his parents in Colombo took precedence

smile and a handshake for the seven-gold Olympic winner Mark Spitz in Cali, Colombia uring the 1975 World championships . . . and talking times with Coach Bill Diaz at liami, 1976.

Power at rest . . . David practising a grab start at Miami, poised and waiting for the signal that will send him into instant action.

understandably and, later, his commitments in the United States had to come first. During his last three competitive years he took part in only two major home meetings, the National championships at Blackpool in July 1974, prior to the European championships in Vienna and the trials for the 1975 Cali World championships, at Crystal Palace in May. He did not race at all in Britain in 1976.

In the summer of 1970, David turned out in a great number of British and Scottish events leading up to the Commonwealth Games, but he missed nearly everything in 1971, partly because of school exams and also because of his summer holiday in Ceylon.

He did compete in the new National short-course championships at Worthing in April of that year when he won his first British titles, two for breaststroke and one for medley. And he was a member of a small Great Britain team of 10 who went on a 17-day showing the flag trip from one side of Canada to the other in July.

Only one serious spell of racing swimming was involved, at the four-day Canadian championships in Edmonton, Alberta. Otherwise, from Halifax to Montreal, Toronto and a Fourth of July Independence Day visit to Niagara Falls, Edmonton, Calgary (to see the famous Stampede) and ending in Vancouver with a cruise down the Fraser river on a $100,000 motor yacht, it was a fun trip, with much kind entertainment and a lot to see.

David was at his most uncooperative, almost boorish — at least that was the impression he succeeded in giving. One Canadian hostess commented somewhat acidly . . . "I thought the British were supposed to have good manners." Her remark was not directed specifically at Wilkie, but he certainly was included.

"I suppose, like many of the team, I was only interested in going along for the trip. I wasn't that concerned about winning in Canada, or even competing. But it was exciting, with so many places to visit and that was what interested me much more than the actual races."

Yet interested in winning or not, David brought off a surprise championships victory at Edmonton. He beat Bill Mahony, the Commonwealth gold medallist who had pushed him into third place in Edinburgh the year before, in the 200 metres breaststroke. Wilkie won by six metres and his 2 min. 32.6 sec. was only one tenth outside his British record. But he was pushed back into third place in the

100 metres breaststroke because he put in an extra short stroke at the finish and he did not reach the final of the 200 metres medley.

It was off to Ceylon immediately after the Canadian trip ended, so he missed British matches in Yugoslavia, West Germany and the Soviet Union — the latter, in Minsk, being against Russia and America. There was no holiday in the sun in 1972 with the Munich Olympics at the end of August. Instead, Harry and Jean Wilkie came to Germany and were lucky enough to see David win his silver.

Wilkie's busiest swimming time was 1973, the year he went to Miami and began to find himself competitively and flex his youthful muscles. In the space of one month, he swam in the N.C.A.A. championships in Knoxville, Tennessee, from March 22nd to 24th, rushed to Pretoria for the South African Games (March 29th-31st), hared back to the United States for the A.A.U. championships in Cincinnati, Ohio (April 4th-7th), returned to Miami for a week, flew to London just in time to join the British team for a Five-Nations contest in Dortmund, West Germany (April 14th-15th) and ended with the Coca-Cola International at Crystal Palace (April 21st-22nd). This involved David in more than 26,000 travelling miles.

He won the N.C.A.A. 200 yards breaststroke title, a very fine effort on this, his first appearance, at this tense, dramatic and highly-competitive meeting, and came fourth in the 100. He was first in his 100 and 200 metres races in Pretoria, but picked up a flu bug there and had to go on antibiotics to get him through the rest of his tough schedule. David lost six pounds in weight as a result and thinks this may have affected his A.A.U. performances in Cincinnati where he had to settle for fifth and third respectively in the 100 and 200 yards events.

He helped Britain to second place behind the host country West Germany in the Dortmund contest, winning the 200 metres breaststroke without difficulty in 2 min. 27.5 sec. but losing out to Walter Kusch of the home team in the 100 metres.

The breaststroke races came out the other way round at the Coca-Cola meeting. David started slowly in the 200 metres and although he pulled back a four-metre deficit with a high-powered sprint over the final lap, he lost to America's Rick Colella, the A.A.U. winner, by a touch. Wilkie's 2 min. 23.8 sec., only a tenth outside his European and Commonwealth records, was in all the circumstances a really pleasing swim.

He was even more delighted on the second day when he beat Mark

Chatfield, the new American sprint champion and Colella over 100 metres. It was another typical Wilkie reaguard effort. He turned more than a body length behind, but won the battle with a flying finish. He clocked 1 min. 6.3 sec., one tenth off his Commonwealth figures, with Chatfield and Colella placed second and third, with the same time of 1:6.7.

Colella and Wilkie clashed again in the 200 metres medley and for once David was ahead at half distance. Then, most unusually, the Scot did not dominate on his breaststroke and the American managed to level, go ahead on freestyle and stay there. Colella returned 2 min. 9.5 sec. while David's 2:10.0, a personal improvement of two and a half seconds, was a Commonwealth mark.

David was pleased with this effort, especially considering his physical condition and the fact that he had not trained properly for three weeks. He had hoped to break that record but believed, eventually, that he could do two or three seconds faster. Wilkie's estimate of his medley potential proved to be very modest. In 1975 he set a World record of 2 min. 6.32 sec. in Vienna and, the next year, at Long Beach, California, trimmed his time to a European and Commonwealth record of 2:6.25 — which proved to be the best in the world in 1976 — in winning the A.A.U. title.

He was very disappointed that the 200 metres medley was left out of the Montreal Olympic events. The International Olympic Committee had demanded that the International Swimming Federation must reduce their programme and the short medley was one of the casualties. David believes the decision was wrong for he considers the 200 metres medley calls for the sort of versatility and all-round ability most compatible with the Olympic ideal — to find the complete sportsman and swimmer. Certainly he must have had a great chance of winning it had the opportunity been there in 1976.

The excitement and glamour of travel, new places and new faces were beginning to pall by the end of 1973 and Wilkie began to think more objectively, more selectively, about his future swimming commitments even though, now and then, he took on more than he could manage. Not being a medal chaser just for the sake of medals, Wilkie saved his efforts for the big occasions. In 1974 these proved to be the Commonwealth Games in Christchurch, the National championships at Blackpool and the European championships in Vienna.

He came back from Miami to swim in the 1975 World championships trials at Crystal Palace in May and did just enough to ensure selection for the 100 and 200 metres breaststroke and 200 metres medley in Colombia.

After the exhausting World championships in Cali in July 1975, David badly needed a rest and the prospect of tackling the eight top nations in the Europa Cup contest in Moscow on August 16th and 17th, two weeks after their long and tiring journey back from Colombia, was not something any of the team looked forward to with enthusiasm. David certainly did not, but the team — and they were Britain's best men's squad in a very long time — needed him for there was even a chance of winning. This *was* an exciting, challenging prospect after a poor record in the previous three contests — seventh and relegated to group B in 1969 and sixth in 1973 having fought back into the A group in 1971.

David went home to Aberdeen for a few days with his family and was scheduled to fly down to London on the morning of departure in good time to connect with the plane to Russia. But there were weather problems in Scotland and his fog-bound flight was delayed for three hours. Eventually, after anxious inquiries about "Where's Wilks?", the rest of the group had to leave without him after team manager Alan Clarkson had arranged for him to follow on the next day.

The weather in Moscow had also changed for the worse, it was bitterly cold, an unseasonable 52 degrees and the contest was to be in the outdoor Lushniki pool in the Lenin Park. For sun-lover David these were daunting, unfavourable conditions.

Clarkson and coach Haller had a problem of how to best allocate the members of their small team, particularly Brian Brinkley, Gordon Downie, Jimmy Carter and Alan McClatchey, around the 12 individual events and three relays in the programme and with a number of unfortunate order of event clashes.

Wilkie was down for three individual events and two relays, Brinkley and Downie also had five, two individual and three relays, Carter four and McClatchey two very important ones.

The British challenge opened with disaster. In the 100 metres freestyle, Downie was "left" on the starting block and finished last. And Carter was only fifth in the 100 metres backstroke. What a start — in more ways than one!

Then came David, whose main breaststroke rival was Nikolay Pankin, Russia's European sprint champion, always a danger man and never more so than when swimming at home. The 100 metres was the first day and although the Briton was lying third at the turn, Pankin could not hold Wilkie and he surged to victory over the second 50 metres in the way only he can do, so powerfully and excitingly.

Brinkley came within centimetres of beating East Germany's European champion Roger Pyttel in the 100 metres butterfly and McClatchey, like Downie and Wilkie, a member of the Warrender club, upheld Scotland's honour by improving four seconds to take third place in the 400 metres freestyle.

The medley relay came next and Carter, Wilkie, Brinkley — with a magnificent butterfly leg — and Downie making up in full measure for his earlier lapse, came within a metre of beating the Soviet Union. After a short break, a weary David dived in for his third race of the night and emerged victorious in the 200 metres medley.

Everyone had tried their best, but the overnight score, with seven events to come on the Sunday, left Britain in third place with 54 points, three behind East Germany, with Russia (79) 25 points ahead.

A pep talk from coach Haller sent the men into battle on the final day in good heart. Wilkie won the 200 metres breaststroke in 2 min. 20.93 sec., the second fastest time in the world that year — and his World championships winning time of 2:18.23 was the fastest.

Brinkley snatched victory in the 200 metres butterfly by one hundredth of a second from Pyttel . . . in the space of 40 minutes Carter took two second places, in the 200 metres backstroke and 400 metres medley . . . and Downie was second in the 200 metres freestyle.

The grand finale was the 4 x 200 metres freestyle relay. And Britain, with McClatchey, Wilkie, who did his best time of 1 min. 58.75 sec. (not bad for a breaststroke swimmer!), Downie and Brinkley came home in first place, three metres ahead of the Soviet Union.

The fighting effort had pulled back 16 points of the over-night deficit and the British squad finished second with 116 points, which was 48 points better than they had ever scored before, to Russia's 125.

The Britons won five out of 15 events, more than any of the other seven nations, and all the victories — of which David had a part in four — were in contest records. Every man had swum the best he knew how, but it was Wilkie and Brinkley in particular — for so long the motivating influences on the team — who had worked their hearts out, who had taken punishment and come up smiling, who had really made it possible.

The Russians named David the "Man of the Match" and at the farewell dinner presented him with a mammoth pumpkin, almost too heavy for one man to carry. With much labour this was brought back to Britain where team boss Clarkson agreed to take it to his home in York in the hope of being able to preserve it for posterity! The history books do not record whether he was successful or not!

David wanted to bow out of swimming on the day of his greatest achievement in Montreal. But his inability to say "no" found him, in the middle of August, 1976, on the way to Pescara on the Adriatic coast for his third and final Europa Cup contest.

The team flew to Rome and then embarked on a four-hour coach ride across the calf of Italy instead of going by plane directly to Pescara. It was a tiresome journey, especially for those who had left home at six in the morning, for the party did not get to their hotel until after 10 at night.

Wilkie had been promised he would not be asked to swim any breaststroke events . . . he did not want to tarnish his golden moment. This pact was kept. He was entered in the 200 metres medley, put down as one of five from whom the 4 x 200 metres free-style relay squad would be chosen and, for the first and last time, was made captain of the British team.

He was up to world record schedule on the first three strokes of the medley, but then his post-Olympic out-of-the-pool activities — receptions, dinners, fetes and being feted — took their toll. He had nothing left on freestyle, Andrey Smirnov of Russia passed him and David, with 2 min. 9.06 sec., finished three seconds off-target in second place.

The race, on August 14, 1976, sadly proved to be Wilkie's last swim for Britain, for Haller decided not to use the Scot, who was not feeling well, in the freestyle relay. Probably, on reflection, David would wish he had stuck to his guns and quit immediately. Yet Haller provides the fitting words:

"David's swimming career finished in Montreal with a gold medal round his neck. But it meant a great deal to the rest of the boys to have him in Pescara and we are all grateful to him . . . certainly I am."

17

DAVID ON COACHES

In gratitude to each and every one

" I realise just how much help I had in preparing for my great moment in Montreal . . . from Charlie Hodgson and Dave Haller, from Coach Diaz, from my parents and friends in Britain and Miami and, of course, the British team. Many people were important in my victory and they should have a share in it.

Unless you count my father in Ceylon, my first coach was Frank Thomas at the Warrender Baths Swimming Club in Edinburgh. I remember, originally, I always called him Mr. Thomas — in fact, at that time, anyone over 20 I either called Sir or Mr. I wasn't exactly scared of him, but I was shy of him. I owe Frank a lot, for he made me develop an interest in swimming — often at great inconvenience to himself — and, if it hadn't been for Frank, I would not be where I am these days.

He was responsible for me from 11 to 16 years of age and I always liked him as a coach. But there must have been many times — those days when I didn't want to swim — when I hated him and he must have been sick to death of me. Then, I would never go training if I could manage to miss it and there were times when Frank used to come to pick me up at school very early in the morning but I never turned up . . . I just stayed in bed. He used to get annoyed at that.

I think I could have developed into a much better swimmer earlier on if I had done all the swimming Frank wanted me to do. But maybe that wouldn't have worked out in the end . . . maybe I'd have been tired of it all before the 1972 Munich Olympics. Maybe my fate was planned that way and it all worked out all right in the end.

As the years went by I responded more to Frank. In fact, there never was a time when I didn't react to him as a coach — when I actually got to the pool. The problem was getting me there! And he was the one who changed my stroke from freestyle to breaststroke.

Even when John Ashton took over the club coaching in 1969, when I was 15, Frank was still there, keeping an eye on things.

John was another big reason why I kept swimming during the two years leading up to the Munich Olympics in 1972. He didn't pressurise me . . . he just sort of made me an offer I couldn't refuse. He said: 'If you keep swimming and do yourself justice, you'll have proved you are a man. And if you don't, you will just have chickened out.'

I enjoyed working with John and I liked him as a person as well as a coach. I went to more training after his arrival and I think I did improve during my time with him.

My next coach was Hammy Bland, the British team coach for the 1972 Olympics in Munich. I was with him for three months, in York, Southampton, Coventry and at the Games, and enjoyed this time. His training was varied, interesting and exciting.

Next came Bill Diaz (the head coach at the University of Miami and known as 'Coach'), from January to March, 1973. I should make the situation clear between myself and Coach. He typified the American approach to swimming and, when I went to Miami, I was the British approach to swimming personified. So I don't think it was easy for Coach to deal with me the first three months, even though I enjoyed working with him for he is a great character and personality.

He found it hard to understand my British attitude and I never really understood his American one. Basically the differences between the two countries were the things that separated us. Coach was always saying what a great country America was . . . always standing up for the States and as I sometimes was critical of America I was critical of him too.

Eventually, Coach and I came to understand that we were different. He represented the blatant American way of life while I, although very changed from the British schoolboy who had crossed the Atlantic in early 1973, still had British backgrounds and British ways of thinking. Coach came from a very poor part of New York City and worked himself into a position of being a really important man in Miami society and a very dedicated man to his sport.

He played a big and influential part in my life and taught me a lot more about my mental approach to swimming than anyone else. His philosophy was that by believing in yourself you can become a good

ying on a champion. The underwater camera eye reveals the secrets of Wilkie's world-
nquering breaststroke technique . . . his strong driving leg-kick, with his big feet
rned outwards . . . his flat streamlined body position . . . the stretching arms and big
nds reaching out to take hold of the water.

Relaxing in Miami — ready for a lobster hunt to make a barbecue lunch on K Biscayne . . . with shapely girl friend Kate Kewley.

The Miami-based Britons — David with Paul Naisby from Sunderland (left) and Welshman Sean Maher who both made the 1976 Olympic team with Wilkie. Scotland's Sandra Dickie was the odd girl out, who didn't make it to Montreal, but with men like these around perhaps she wasn't too unhappy.

person and also a good swimmer. He was very positive in everything he did and I have a lot to thank him for. And Coach was always there when I needed him . . . if I had any problems.

Then came Charlie Hodgson, a former butterflyer and a great technique man. He dashed up to Montreal for the 200 metres after seeing on television something wrong in my stroke. Under him I reached my full potential technically.

He would get into the water and try out stroke ideas and he really did help me. He was the man who changed my stroke just before the World championships in Cali in 1975. He wasn't pushy, just interested in what you were doing and very interesting to work with. Charlie looked after me until just before the 1976 Olympics when Dave Haller, as British team coach, took over.

Dave had been my coach each summer for a few weeks before each big competition. He always played an important part in my success. He set my tapers, charged my mental approach before I swam . . . so he had the biggest influence on me in the most important way. I had a lot of faith in him and that is very important . . . if you don't have faith, then a coach cannot guide you.

He and Charlie are completely different in some respects yet very similar in lots of others. Dave is a confident person who doesn't show his confidence. Charlie is always giving you target times which are impossible, but he never lets on afterwards whether the times he set were serious or not. Dave tells you the times he thinks you can do — which are slower than the times I think I can do. So with Dave saying a time in direct opposition to Charlie — a second slower than I'm thinking and Charlie a second faster — I was the guy in the middle who had to do it!

Because swimmers in America are so competitive, Charlie used to theorise about the need to have the killer instinct. I wouldn't exactly go along with that, but certainly he taught me to be hard and not let anyone intimidate me.

Will I become a swimming coach one day? I am not sure I would be any good at it, even though I have been coached by some of the greatest coaches in Britain and America. It doesn't follow that because someone is a good swimmer, even an Olympic champion, he would be able to produce good swimmers. But if I did ever become a coach, I think I'd be quite hard. In my experience, youngsters are perceptive, willing to learn and respond to a positive approach.

It must be in the back of the mind of a person who wins a medal at an Olympic Games that he would like to train an Olympic champion himself. But there aren't many Olympic champions who return to the sport and do this. So, all I can say is I think I would like to coach when I have settled down and got my future straightened out . . . but I don't think I'll have time to even think about this for a few years."

18

COACHES ON DAVID

Unique is the word

Just as Wilkie has his own opinions of coaches, they too have their ideas about him. Two men vitally concerned in David's world-wide achievements are Charlie Hodgson, who prepared the Scot in the United States for his medal-crowned triumphs in Vienna, Cali and Montreal, and Dave Haller, who coached the British men's team to their successes at World and European championships and the 1976 Olympic Games.

Charlie was born in Miami in 1947 and swam competitively from the age of nine to 21. He graduated from Dartmouth College with a Bachelor of Arts degree in 1969 and a Bachelor of Engineering in 1970, then served as a 1st Lieutenant in the U.S. Army for three years. He coached part time from 1970 to 1973 when he gave up career ideas of being an engineer, working indoors under depressing flourescent lighting, for the sunshine of Florida and the chance of coaching talented swimmers at the University of Miami. This is what Hodgson has to say about his relationship with Wilkie:

"In a nutshell, David Wilkie is an intelligent, determined, disciplined, quiet, controlled, highly-talented competitor. He is intelligent in his ability to learn from everyone and decipher the useful information from the not so useful. He is determined in his drive to reach his ultimate potential and knows his capabilities. He is disciplined in his training and habits. He is quiet and somewhat secretive in most situations. And he is controlled in his emotions, as he showed by his calmness on winning his gold medal in Montreal.

David is also endowed with tremendous swimming talent which is obvious to anyone who watches him. There is probably no one more coachable and because of his great feel for the water and open-mindedness towards changes, he is able to experiment with his stroke most successfully. He almost never has to be pushed in work-outs because he is always pushing himself. And he takes excellent care of his health and avoids activities which might risk the chance of injury.

These are the attributes that make David a phenomenal athlete —great and that greatness will carry over from swimming to whatever course of life he pursues.

There are several reasons why David and I worked well together, but the main one is that he believed in me and I believed in him. Never was there any doubt in my mind that David Wilkie could and would be the greatest breaststroke swimmer the world had ever seen. This unwavering faith had to be evident to him and it was also obvious that I wanted to be his main coach.

I liked him and enjoyed working with him and I think David enjoyed working with me because I was always positive, always tried to challenge and stimulate him with new ideas and different ways of training. I tried to keep him informed about his competitions and always paid attention to stroke detail during work-outs and constantly emphasised the importance of perfect form. Finally, I think David knew I was sincerely interested in him.

My philosophy is never to establish unrealistic times as challenging goals for athletes and my aim in setting times is to bring out the full potential in a swimmer. Those I set for David at the Montreal Olympics were totally realistic.

The exact times I established two months before the Games were 1 min. 2.6 sec. for 100 metres breaststroke and 2 min. 15.0 sec. for 200 metres. Having observed and trained David for three years, I believed, without doubt, that he was fully capable of these times and, if achieved, he would reach his full potential.

The 100 metres time was absolutely *not* impossible. Remember, David did a 1:3.43 in the final (John Hencken won in 1:3.11), despite losing between six to eight tenths of a second on his start, when he took off at a bad angle and, as a result, his feet came out of the water and he obtained almost zero propulsion from his first leg kick. This is why David was half a body length behind at the beginning of the 100 metres final.

After David had beaten Hencken in both A.A.U. breaststroke championships at Long Beach (April 1976) I wrote: 'Only

Montreal remains to determine whether David will reach his full potential'. The day after David won the 200 metres gold medal, I had a short chat with him and he made a telling remark, the meaning of which was not obvious to me until several days later.

David said: 'I'm happy with the time because I think I reached my full potential.' I never realized how terribly important, maybe more important than getting the gold, it was to David to reach his full potential. **"**

Haller, a former Olympic freestyle sprinter, is big enough to rival any of his lads for sheer size and bulk. He gives the impression of a genial grizzly bear, with a roar to match. Smiling and easy-going he may be on the surface, but hard-man Haller does not miss much and he is stern and shrewd, too. Here is coach Haller's verdict on swimmer Wilkie:

"David is a unique person. He is natural, relaxed, gentle and not a bit aggressive, until it comes to his swimming, and he has the strength, character and courage to pull himself through difficulties. That is why he is such a great competitor.

He is very easy to coach and he is concerned that the parts others play in his success are given proper recognition. David talks quietly and listens and consults about his swimming and he is remarkably cool under pressure.

Yet for all his success he is very modest, doesn't feel he is superior and has never asked for or expected special treatment. He doesn't think he should be on a pedestal and the rest of the squad don't put him on that lofty pinnacle.

He is a great member of the team, even though he does what he has to do for his own swimming and likes to hibernate for his own events. He is also very involved in all aspects of what the others are doing and because of his involvement everyone has benefited, particularly the less experienced ones. At the 1974 European championships, for example, he really helped young Gordon Hewit. The two shared a room and I went in one day and found David had put a big notice on the wall which read: 'WINNING ISN'T EVERYTHING — IT'S THE ONLY THING.'

One of his great assets is the ability to know what is important and what is not. So, he doesn't expect or try to be on peak form the whole year round, for he knows what his big targets are and he doesn't worry about what his rivals are doing in between. David probably only swims really well for about 15 minutes a year, WHEN IT MATTERS.

He goes for the one BIG effort at a time and finds it difficult to recharge — it is part of his defence mechanism, because he concentrates so intensely. And this is why he has sometimes not won events he was expected to win.

The mental discipline required for swimming breaststroke is far greater than for any of the other three styles. The swimmer must have superb technique and be able to relax. He must not rush, allow his stroking to be hurried, and that requires control of the highest order. David has this mental discipline, along with an ideal breaststroke physique . . . a highly-floatable lean body, long limbs, powerful leg muscles and supple ankles. All these things make him the superb champion he is."

19

TECHNIQUE

Most important of all

The one thing in swimming that David Wilkie is absolutely certain about is the paramount importance of technique. This applies particularly to those who swim breaststroke; which, technically, is the most difficult and complicated stroke of all and whose rules are more precise than those of backstroke, butterfly and freestyle put together.

David started life with four prime assets for swimming success . . two big hands and two big feet. And he grew up to be long-limbed, broad-shouldered and slim-hipped — the perfect streamlined shape for a swimming champion.

Another talent and one that must have been seen by Warrender club coach Frank Thomas, during the years between 1966 and 1972 when he fought to keep David swimming, was a natural feel for water — that challenging element, as David describes it.

"I spent most of my life in places near rivers or the sea so water always was attractive. But it challenges . . . and you are always fighting it . . . you can never stop, or you will drown. This constant battle with the element is something not be found on land."

Once our reluctant champion had found pleasure and satisfaction in the disciplines of training, the challenging element, so magnetic to him in his young days, became something he could bend to his will.

Wilkie, originally a moderate freestyler, who drifted into breast-stroke in 1969, developed a most unorthodox but effective stroke and he kept this up until 1975. He used to pull his arms inside his shoulder-line towards his chest, his fingers pointed towards his chest as he drew his hands back and then recovering just under his chin. With it he became World, European and Commonwealth champion and world record holder.

In April 1975, when Miami coach Charlie Hodgson was searching for more and more speed, he asked David to change a habit of a swimming life-time and adopt a new arm action and Wilkie, always prepared to take advice, agreed without a qualm.

The change involved adopting an orthodox pull, in which the hands move in a circular sweep outside the shoulder-line and then come back under the shoulder-line for the recovery. Now the fingers pointed forwards all the time and, on the pull back, the palms swept sideways.

"It amounted to a shortening of my pull and, although for a few months it felt strange, once I got used to it I found it much easier to swim that way."

The international rules for breaststroke say that:

(a) The body shall be kept perfectly on the breast and both shoulders shall be in line with the water surface from the beginning of the first arm stroke after the start and on the turn.

(b) All movements of the legs and arms shall be simultaneous and in the same horizontal plane without alternating movement.

(c) The hands shall be pushed forward together from the breast, and shall be brought back on or under the surface of the water.

(d) In the leg kick the feet shall be turned outwards in the backward movement. A "dolphin" kick (i.e. an up and down flutter kick) is not permitted.

(e) At the turn and upon finishing the race, the touch shall be made with both hands simultaneously at the same level, either at, above or below the water level.

(f) A part of the head shall always be above the general water level, except that at the start and at each turn the swimmer may take one arm stroke and one leg kick while wholly submerged.

vid's greatest moment, the one he had waited for after his golden 200 metres breast-
oke victory in Montreal — when he saw his world record-breaking 2 min. 15.11 sec. on
scoreboard. Then it was triumph and the arms go up in glory and delight.

Joy day for Jean Wilkie — to be with her son David in Montreal. (Courtesy Monte Fres *Daily Mirror.)*

Within three months, at the World championships in Cali in July, David had improved his 100 metres time by 1½ seconds and his 200 metres best by one second to win both titles in European and Commonwealth record times, only just outside the world records.

Dave Haller, Wilkie's British team coach for four years, clarified the changes succinctly:

"David's technique is based around a very strong leg kick, because of his large feet and very good flexibility of legs and ankles. He has a unique ability to accelerate his leg kick without losing the feel of the water and so he is able to apply full power through his leg action. Because of his natural body streamlining and his flat position in the water, David's new arm action gave him an increase in basic speed and the ability to hold his stroke over the longer distances. Also it helped him to make more effective use of his shoulder and back muscles.

"Wilkie's magnificent, surging leg-kick technique is almost the perfect breaststroke style. Conversely, David's great rival John Hencken, who also is a near-perfect exponent of the stroke, is an arms man. He has a powerful upper body, but his leg-kick is nothing like as strong as Wilkie's.

"Arm-men have more basic speed . . . leg-men can go further. If Hencken had Wilkie's legs, or vice-versa, you would have absolute perfection in breaststroke."

David's explanation is similar yet different:

"John relies on his arms; I rely on my legs. The leg muscles need more oxygen and therefore tire more quickly, but they produce more power so that evens things out. In the end, it is all down to who is the fitter overall."

At the Montreal Olympics, arm-man Hencken out-sprinted Wilkie over 100 metres, but leg-man David soundly trounced the American in the 200. So, on the face of it both Haller and Wilkie are right.

In Wilkie's view, Mark Spitz, the history-making winner of a record seven gold medals at the Munich Olympics of 1972, is the most perfect technician in any stroke he has ever seen. David says this even though he was furious with the tactless American in Montreal for publicly tipping Hencken to win the 200 metres — a forecast that brought an equally-loud rejoinder of "No way" from one forthright Briton present.

"Mike Bruner (the American who won the 200 metres butterfly in Montreal in a world record sub-two minute time) was much stronger and tremendously fit. Even so, because of his perfect style and technique, Spitz was swimming the 200 nearly as fast as Bruner four years earlier and the 100 metres butterfly record he set in Munich was the only one not beaten during the men's events in Montreal.

"And look at the East German women (who won all but two of their titles in Montreal), they have lots of strength and are very flexible. But, above all, they have superb technique. When East Germany started their great swimming build-up, the first thing their coaches did was to study all the best swimmers in the world to find out what aspects of technique had made them successful, then they used that knowledge to improve their own swimmers.

"That is why the East German girls are so far ahead now. It is no good the rest of the world dismissing them as just power girls. They should look at Kornelia Ender (winner of a record four gold medals in Montreal) and study her.

"The difference between the American men (who won every title in Montreal — except for the ONE you-know-who took) and the East German women boils down to the difference in training methods. The U.S. men work on strength and endurance. The East German women, building on a foundation of fitness, then concentrate on flexibility and technique. It cannot be emphasised enough that learning the right techniques is of first importance.

"Of course, the East Germans are selective about the people they put into swimming. You'll find that, like me, their stars mostly have big feet and big hands. Obviously you can swim faster with a pair of natural (size 10½) flippers!

"Tiny technical alterations in my stroke — you could call them refinements — came about in 1976, probably because all the training I had been doing had got me into really good condition. So my body became very relaxed in the water and I was able to stretch just a little bit more. Before my stroke had been slightly more compact because my body was tighter. But it was all involuntary . . . it wasn't planned, it just happened, perfection coming from maturity perhaps?"

A great Wilkie attribute was his ability to change effortlessly from what he called his 100 metres to his 200 metres stroke. It was something he did constantly in training, something he dismissed almost casually, saying all it involved was pulling deeper and longer and with a bigger stretch for the 200 metres stroke.

In fact, he used his 200 stroke for the first half of his 100 metres race in Montreal. It was easier, did not tire him and, as a result, he was able to come back extremely fast on the last 50 metres.

That event caused some concern to Haller and Charlie Hodgson, who came up from Miami having seen Wilkie in action on television, that their star man was revving a bit too fast — using his arms too much. Haller certainly wanted Wilkie to take the 200 much more steadily and he did, most effectively!

Once David had set his mind on becoming the best breaststroke swimmer in the world, he found that the loneliness of long distance training, spending anything up to 30 hours a week in the water, suited his sometimes solitary disposition.

"When you are in the pool you can't speak to others, there is no contact and you have to have a high degree of concentration on what you are doing . . . whether it is kicking holding a float, endurance work, sprints, specialised stroke drills to practise various aspects, starts or turns. This is what I have always liked about training. It is like an escape and nobody can bother you.

"I know people say that to churn up and down a pool for hours on end is a mindless thing to do. If you are mindless to start with, I suppose that would be true. But I regard it as four hours a day of intense thought and concentration and I don't know what I shall do, now, without it.

"What do I think about? My thoughts wander and I find myself thinking of all sorts of things, most of them too personal to be discussed with anybody. In those moments I am honest with myself."

One swimming hazard which David has kept very much to himself is his allergy to chlorinated water, which for someone spending one quarter of his waking life in such an element must have been a huge burden.

"Chlorinated water makes me itch. It gives me a chronic cold all the time . . . sniffles, a blocked nose and sneezing bouts. But nobody has come up with a cure and I've learned to live with it."

David, mentally, quit swimming on July 24th, 1976, the moment his hands touched the end of the Montreal pool after 2 min. 15.11 sec. of magnificent breaststroke swimming which made him

Olympic champion and world record-holder. And though he was persuaded, probably against his better inclinations, to be in the British team for the Europa Cup match two weeks later in Pescara, Italy, it is very likely he regretted making this final gesture.

Yet, at only 22, he could have gone on swimming for several more years, like Russia's 27-year-old Nikolay Pankin and the 25-year-olds Roland Matthes of East Germany and Nobutaka Taguchi of Japan.

So why did Wilkie decide this was the end, that enough was enough? "If I had gone on, the only way to improve would have been to work harder and harder and there comes a point when you cannot give any more of your time." And even for a young man, time cannot be devoted, for ever, to sport. For the future beckons.

Typical Wilkie Work-outs at the University of Miami
(1975-76 winter season)

October (five a week) — Monday, Wednesday and Friday afternoons, short-course (25-yard pool), and Tuesday and Thursday mornings, long-course (50-metre pool).

Short-course (4,500 yards)

500 yd. medley

500 yd. backstroke, pulling

12 x 75 yd. pull on 1 min. 15 sec. (three on each stroke)

500 yd. easy

15 min. exergenie work (local muscular endurance exercises, using pulleys)

3 x 500 yd. starting every 6 min. 15 sec.

48 x 12½ yd. on 20 sec. without breathing

Long-course (5,000 metres)

400 m. freestyle — 300 m. backstroke — 300 m. breaststroke — 300 m. butterfly

500 m. kicking

4 x 50 m. breaststroke underwater with only three breaths, starting every 1½ min.

4 x 400 m. freestyle with negative splits (i.e. swimming the end faster than the beginning) on 7½ min.

600 m. stroke drills (unusual variations of sectional work)

4 x 200 m. breaststroke, negative split, on 4 min.

November and December (seven a week) — Monday to Friday after-noons, short-course, and Tuesday and Thursday mornings, long-course.

Short-course (6,900 yards)

1,000 yd. swim, changing strokes
500 yd. kicking
3 x 200 yd. kick on 3½ min.
2 x 100 yd. kick on 1½ min.
8 x 25 yd. kick on 30 sec.
16 x 25 yd. underwater on 35 sec.
5 x 200 yd. broken swims, resting at 50 yd. on 4 min. 10 sec.
1,000 yd. swim, working turns hard
5 x 100 yd. on 1 min. 30 sec., pulling
5 x 100 yd. on 1 min. 25 sec., pulling
5 x 100 yd. on 1 min. 20 sec.
5 x 100 yd. on 1 min. 15 sec.

Long-course (6,000 metres)

50 m. butterfly — 100 m. backstroke — 150 m. breaststroke — 200 m. freestyle — 250 m. butterfly — 300 m. backstroke — 350 m. breaststroke — 400 m. freestyle (total 1,800 metres)
600 m. kicking (alternating slow and fast kicks)
8 x 100 m. kicking on 1 min. 45 sec.
800 m. breaststroke, pulling
200 m. on 3 min. and 100 m. on 1½ min. (repeated five times without rest)
2 x 50 m. on 1 min.

January and February (11 a week) — Monday to Saturday after-noons, short-course, and Monday, Tuesday and Thursday to Satur-day mornings, long-course.

Short-course (6,000 yards)

4 x 375 yd. on 5½ min.
5 x 125 yd. on 2 min. 15 sec.
5 x 175 yd. breaststroke pull on 3½ min.
10 x 25 yd. swimming without breathing on 30 sec.
9 x 50 yd. freestyle on 40 sec.
5 x 400 yd. kicking on 6½ min.
300 yd. swim down (i.e. relaxing off)

Long-course (5,000 metres)

700 m. swim

10 x 50 m. kicking on 1 min.

5 x 200 m. medley (reverse order) on 3 min. 15 sec.

6 x 200 m. on 3 min.

10 x 100 m. on 1 min. 40 sec. (alternating fast and slow)

2 x 50 m. for speed

March (taper time) — a typical short-course work-out 10 days before the N.C.A.A. championships.

Short-course (2,000 yards)

4 x 100 yd. on 1½ min. descending (taking each one faster than the previous one and with the final one flat out)

6 x 50 yd. on 1 min. descending

100 yd. swim

4 x 50 yd. breaststroke on 1 min. descending

1 x 200 yd. breaststroke, broken by 10 sec. rest at each 50 yd. (all-out, with three pulse checks every 30 sec. after finish)

100 yd. swim

3 x 200 yd. freestyle, negative split, on 3 min. 15 sec.

100 yd. swim down

20

MIAMI

Four years I shall never forget

David went to the University of Miami in January 1973 having been recruited provisionally before Munich and been very much in demand after he had won his Olympic silver in the 200 metres breast-stroke. To the young man, 18 years old and just out of school, the offer of a substantial scholarship, a place in the sun, a chance to train in the open-air all the year round, go snorkling on the Florida Keys, was all very glamorous and exciting — even if there were classes, lectures and studying along with the good swimming prospects.

Many offers of scholarships had come from American universities after Munich — from the University of Southern California at Los Angeles and from Indiana and Harvard — but Miami had an extra-special lure, a top-level course in marine biology, in which David was very interested. And the Florida university astutely clinched their offer by inviting Wilkie out, a month after the Games, to see if he liked what he saw. And he looked, and he saw and he went.

"Even before Munich I had decided I did want to go to America and although other universities were interested, I went to Miami and, looking back, I have had four years that I shall never forget. I enjoyed my swimming there, my life there and the people I met.

Miami is a university where people go to enjoy themselves . . . the beautiful weather, lovely surroundings and the sea. It's also an expensive place for it costs on an average $6,000 a year for school-ing, housing, food and incidentals.

The total value of my scholarship, which was a full one, was $22,000 for the time I was there. I know many people thought when I got this I was in the money. Actually, I didn't touch a cent for it all went directly to pay for my tuition, books, room, board and laundry.

Sports scholarships in America are governed by the rules of the National Collegiate Athletic Association and depend upon your ability as a competitor. The better you are the greater chance you have of receiving a full scholarship. Under N.C.A.A. rules, each university can only give four full swimming scholarships a year and cannot have more than 10 in operation at any one time. Thus, if eight people are on returning scholarships at the beginning of a semester, only two more can be offered.

Most American students are allowed to do part-time work, to help pay for their education, unless they are receiving full grants. Then they cannot work in term time, but may do so in the vacations. As a foreigner, I wasn't allowed to work at all. The immigration officers are very strict about this and if they do find you working they would deport you. And I didn't want that.

So I couldn't work to help pay for the incidentals, toothpaste, shaving cream, the odd beer, bus fares if I had a chance to go to the beach, clothing and all the miscellaneous things. My parents helped, I had a bit of money of my own, and some of my friends around the Miami area made sure I didn't starve. So I never really did worry about money until it came to the build-up for Montreal.

I wanted to stay on in Miami in the summer of 1976 to prepare for the Games, but my scholarship was running out. Then Alan Weeks, the Director of the Sports Aid Foundation, which had recently been set up in London, came to Florida in March (to do a television programme on David for the B.B.C.). When he discovered my problem, he promised to see what he could do.

He helped me put in a request via the British A.S.A. and a short time after he let me know that the Foundation had allowed me £450 to cover lodging, eating, training and medical treatment for the two months before I joined the British team in Canada.

This was terrific and I thought it would have been enough. But I had made a few miscalculations in my application. I forgot I would need petrol to drive to and from practice each day . . . and the cost of the protein powder and vitamins I was taking . . . and the kind of good food (and therefore expensive) I was trying to eat to get my body in shape for the Games.

Worst of all, I never thought about the possible drop in the value of the £ sterling against the dollar. From the time I made my application until I got the money, I think the dollar went from 2.10 to 1.80 to the £, which worked out at $135 (or 14 per cent) less than I had budgeted for.

I got exactly what I asked for, so I have no complaints and with this help I knew I could afford to stay somewhere comfortable, eat nutritious food instead of hamburgers and not worry where my next meal was coming from. It was a kind gesture and at the right time. It took one worry off my pre-Montreal preparations and I was most grateful. The only other money I've ever received to help with training was £50 from the city of Edinburgh before the 1972 Munich Olympics.

By the time I left Aberdeen, after the 1973 New Year, I think I had matured quite a lot because of what happened in Munich. Even so, my first year in Miami was one of adjustment. The social differences were quite vast, the people were different, and I had to gear myself up for the American way of life. The first year wasn't a bed of roses and I had some problems. But because I didn't have any ties I was able to give most of my nervous energy to swimming.

There were lots of pluses and minuses in being at Miami but the sum added up to me having the best chance I could to do well at swimming and get a fine education. On the good side, we only used to go training once a day at week-ends, so there was a chance for socialising . . . sailing, fishing, visiting friends. And meeting different people, seeing different places and learning about different cultures is something I can thank Miami and my swimming career for.

Inevitably, because I wanted to become a champion swimmer, there were things that had to be given up . . . perhaps not to a great extent but a restriction on things one would enjoy doing. During training we were never allowed to drink or stay up late — common sense if you have to be up at seven to go to the pool. And we had to miss the best part of the day on the beach because we were training again from 2 till 4 in the afternoon. But if a swimmer can reach the top, then all the work and little giving-ups are worth while.

Top athletes get the chance of a better education in the United States than they would anywhere else, because the teachers and professors treat them more individually and make allowances. The system is used to athletes taking a week off from studies here and there and they are prepared to vary the types of examinations they set or move the dates of them, within reason, to avoid a clash with sporting fixtures. This would never have been possible in Britain.

At Miami, too, everything is geared towards the competitors; they try to instil purpose into their training programme and there is a pride to be on the squad. When we have a meet, there is excitement, everyone is there to win, to do a good job and everybody shouts and cheers the team. It was like being back at Warrender.

The university teams are known as the Hurricanes — because Miami lies within a hurricane belt and the university was nearly destroyed by one the year after it was built in 1926.

We wear green track suits, with orange and white stripes and Miami on the front and Hurricanes on the back. When we come out before a match, we rush through an arch of what looks like white smoke — it's harmless gas. There's a record blaring out crowd noises, shouts and applause, as we run down the pool-side and gather in a circle. We have two cheer leaders and our shout is 'Here comes a knife . . . yea, yea.' And, yea, yea, it really gets the team going. **"**

This team feeling is something Wilkie enjoys, as does the man behind the Hurricanes, the 50-year-old Puerto Rican from New York, Bill Diaz. It was Coach Diaz who made the first approach to David, through Tyrone "Tarzan" Tozer, the Miami-based South African, who was one of Diaz's original recruits. Coach was responsible for bringing the Scot over for his inspection week-end but it was Tozer and another South African, Robert van der Mere, who put the gloss on the trip.

"I was overwhelmed by my reception at the airport. Robert came in his own E-type Jaguar while Tyrone had a borrowed Corvette I suppose I should have realised it was a bit much but, frankly, I was impressed. They gave me a hectic social time — I think they had planned it that way."

By the end of it, Diaz had got his man even though his contact with his star-to-be was a few words and a hand-shake. Wilkie, in fact, was the first Miami Briton although the trickle turned into a stream. Sean Maher from Wales arrived in February 1974 and Sunderland's Paul Naisby, the Commonwealth breaststroke double bronze medallist, followed in September that year.

Scotland's Sandra Dickie was there for a spell and by the start of the 1976/77 academic year, the British contingent had been reinforced by Gary Abraham, Kevin Burns, Duncan Cleworth and Peter erpiniere, all members of the British Olympic team in Montreal.

In fact, the Britons are popular in Miami and with Coach. As David said: "I think the university gets more value from the British wimmers."

At the beginning, Coach Diaz was as baffled by Wilkie as the Scot was with the whole American scene. Coach was quoted as aying: "He's different — super intelligent — he's a definite puzzle, ut I'm working on it. Give me time." And, in time, the extrovert Latin-American and the quiet Scot with his very British attitude did arrive at a working understanding, though never a total comprehension.

"Coach was a father figure to me. And he was a tremendous influence. He was very concerned about our welfare . . . making the best arrangements for us on trips . . . and when we were away at the N.C.A.A. or the A.A.U. meetings and there was only a $7-a-day budget for food — which isn't very much — he'd be prepared to buy us a dinner if we looked starving! I always found him very generous."

But even Diaz couldn't finance the annual New Year training trips to Jamaica (1974), Puerto Rico (1975) and Cali, Colombia, in 1976. It meant that the squad members had to raise, individually, the cost of their air fares, anything up to $250, through sponsorship. The swimmers would go out and knock on doors, telling people who they were and what they did, asking for help on a sponsored swim so that the university team could carry through Coach's programme.

David more than justified Miami's faith in him. He never lost a 200 yards race in a college dual meet the whole time he was in America and he went on to become the university's first and only Olympic champion in any sport.

Though it is true that ability in sport can give athletes the opportunity of a free education, they, in turn, by representing their university in competition, can promote the image of the institution.

"Wherever I went to swim throughout the world, the name 'University of Miami' appeared. They were very well aware of this and they are very thankful towards me for it. The university paper voted me the outstanding athlete three years in succession, in 1973, 74 and 75 (and surely 1976 too!). The Miami Hurricane also vote for the 'Athlete of the Quarter of a Century' and the sport editor wrote that maybe 'in 25 years from now David Wilkie will be the one' . . . but 2000 AD is a bit far to think about!

"Miami even put on a 'David Wilkie Day' in honour of my Montreal gold medal and for spreading the good name of the university around the country. It was very embarrassing walking round the campus seeing all those signs saying 'Honour David Wilkie' . . . 'Come to the Pool to see Wilkie'. It was like a whole day dedicated to me . . . all very American, but it warmed the cockles of my heart . . . very nice."

The ceremonies at the pool took two hours and it was quite a show. There were hot-dogs on sale, a band and a model parade. All the dignitaries of the university were invited. And the climax came with the presentation by the President of the University, Henry King Stanford, of a huge wooden plaque with David's picture on it etched in metal and a record of all his achievements.

Though David retired from competition after Montreal, old habits die hard.

"I went down to the pool to watch my friends, my old team-mates, training. And I went to the lane I used to swim in and I was kind of looking to see where I was, how I was doing — and it really felt strange when I discovered I wasn't there. I said to the boys afterwards, 'Phew, that was a hard work-out!' and they said, 'Go to hell!' "

21

BETTER BRITAIN

The facts of swimming life

What follows now may make unpalatable, unpatriotic or down-right unpleasant reading for those who run sport in this country. But the truth, plain and unvarnished, is always hard to swallow and in its direct and forceful way can be something many people try to avoid at all costs. And let there be no accusations of lack of patriotic spirit about this man Wilkie for his pride in swimming and winning for Britain in Montreal was obvious — and proudly stated too.

Yet it is impossible to get away from the underlying frustration and sadness in what Wilkie says about the British scene — and there is a hell of a lot of sense too. David is not the mindless moron that many people think a swimming champion must be . . . churning up and down a pool for hours a day, all alone, in a strip of water, in a conversationless vacuum. He is not the unthinking automaton that authority in Britain would like their competitors to be. Nor is he destructively critical but constructively helpful when he talks about how it could and should be.

David has had experience of swimming in both Britain and America. If he comes down in favour of the United States set-up, and would like people in Britain to know how it is across the Atlantic, his opinions do not have to be liked but they do have to be respected. So before Britain becomes too dizzy as a result of basking in the reflected glory of Wilkie's gold medals from Olympic, World, European and Commonwealth competitions, two indisputable home truths should be swallowed along with the celebratory champagne.

If David had not gone to America in January 1973 to train and study, he almost certainly would have been out of swimming within a year.

And if he had struggled along under the British system, he neve would have achieved the world honours, medals, records and glor that have come as a result of his four years at the University o Miami, in Florida, U.S.A.

" I had to leave Britain to continue at high level. And I'm glad tha I made that decision — otherwise all I might have achieved woul have been that silver medal from the Munich Olympics.

If I had stayed I might have continued for a year but then I migh well have fallen into the same traps as I did in my early days in Scot land . . . losing interest, skipping training . . . dropping out. And if had gone to college in Scotland, I would have been too busy studyin to keep swimming.

There isn't the level of competition in Britain that there is in th United States — not the week-by-week clashes against a lot of goo swimmers. The whole American system is highly competitive, eve the training. That's the sort of competition to keep you interested a well as in trim.

So even if I could have trained in Britain as I did in Miami, I don think I would have succeeded in the world sense, purely because o the lack of this class of competition . . . lack of motivation.

There is only one real answer. Britain ought to set up sponsore areas, based on the few full-time professional coaches, wher swimmers from different localities can be regrouped.

The swimmers could go to school, college or university, yet atten a swim club with a good coach — as the countries in Eastern Europe like East Germany, the Soviet Union and Hungary, etc., have don for years. In fact, like Britain did before the 1972 Olympics, when training scheme was set up in York. The competitors were foun jobs or had their education organised, where we stayed with familie who were interested in what we were doing. I know that was onl temporary but that's the principle.

Good swimmers should go where there are good coaches. I seemed to work very well at York and I think most of the peopl there were happy, enjoyed themselves and swam well.

I am sure a lot of people would find it hard to leave home — bu Britain is a small country and it would not be difficult to go hom some week-ends or for parents to visit their children. It all depend how much you want to be a success.

It would require somebody to sponsor the people until they go settled down. The amount of money it would take . . . ? Well, mo schooling is free in this country — and people going to university mostly can go there free too, with grants. And I am sure the universities could help out, with scholarships and also with training. And something could be worked out with the school authorities, so the swimmers could start an hour later and get their training in before they go to school, if necessary stay on later or do extra home-work.

For swimmers really to fulfil their potential and begin to learn what it is all about, you have got to have groups of good ones training together competitively. To leave people dotted around the country because of the circumstances of where their homes are is not the way to produce champions. And in fulfilling their swimming potential they can also begin to fulfil their life's potential too.

A concept like this, which involves more than just swimming, would have to have the support and understanding of the individual coaches, who would have to be mature and honest enough to realise, for whatever the circumstance, when they are not able to give their swimmers everything they need.

And the jealousies would have to be overcome. Because one coach may not like another, personally, this shouldn't be a bar to accepting the rival as a good coach. The right thoughts should be 'my swimmers will benefit and for this reason I would like them to go'.

This would take a lot of organising, of course, and the responsibility should not fall on the shoulders of the coaches. It would need a team of helpers . . . to solve the problems of jobs or education, accommodation and finance. But it could be done and I believe it must be done. Maybe it would even help to keep swimmers in the sport.

Maybe swimming could persuade business and industry to get involved in the grass roots production of good swimmers . . . like sponsoring swim-school set-ups, say British Leyland at Coventry, Bells Whisky at Stirling in Scotland or Coca-Cola, who already support a swim meet. The school-swim centre competitors could be provided with track suits which give the names of the sponsors, so that the companies, who are not just philanthropists, could get some commercial return.

I know that the Sports Aid Foundation has been formed to help outstanding individuals, potential champions, to prepare for the big events. But swimming champions do not often emerge from individual situations, training by themselves against the clock. They come out of competitive training groups, where there is constant man-to-man (woman-to-woman) pressure throughout the whole of the year under the supervision of top quality coaches, such as the one I was lucky enough to be in at Miami. And this fact is something that has never been put over properly, so far as I understand, to those who are trying to help Britain to the top of the sporting tree.

The Brian Brinkley situation at Bedford provides a good illustration of how Britain misses out. I know Brian, captain of the British team, did fantastically well, winning Commonwealth, European, World and Olympic medals, but only one was a gold, a Commonwealth Games one. Yet all his swimming life, except when he was away with teams, he had to train virtually by himself against the clock. And that's no damn good, it's soul-destroying . . . and the prospect of having to do what Brian was doing was one reason why I had to get OUT and go to America.

Yet, if Brian had been with a bunch of good swimmers of his calibre all the time, it would not have been so hard for him. All he needed to be right on the top of the world was the killer instinct — the umph to get in there. He had the will to win, and he did unbelievable things in relay squads, but he didn't know how to win individually. He would have learned that with a competitive group.

In America you are training with those damn people, who are trying to beat you and you are racing against them all the time. In Miami, if you get beaten in training, the squad give you a hard time and the coach gives you a hard time. It is all done on purpose . . . getting on each other's backs. But Brian didn't have that — all he had was his coach. And you can get sick and tired of hearing the coach saving 'faster, faster . . . harder, harder'.

If you practice swimming against good people all the time, you practice mental strength day in and day out. And this helps when it matters. You know exactly what is needed to win and you learn to overcome the difficulties, mental and physical.

I think some new national philosophy is the only answer now, otherwise we are going to continue with our club level competitions and horizons which don't mean much in terms of the big time.

England, Scotland and Wales all have their competitions and then there are the events for Great Britain. To be honest, lots of these meets are a waste of time and the dates are often placed in such a a way that they don't build up to anything. It is hard to get anything out of them — except some pleasant trips abroad, which cut across training. And they don't lead anywhere and there is no pattern to the programme.

...way from the blocks for the 100 metres breaststroke final (top to bottom) *Arvidas ozaytis* (U.S.S.R.) *almost hidden, third; Giorgio Lalle* (Italy), *fifth; Walter Kusch* (West *ermany), sixth; John Hencken* (U.S.A.), *first; Graham Smith* (Canada), *fourth; David ilkie, second, and Duncan Goodhew* (G.B.), *seventh . . . and* (below) *in full flight.*

1

"May I introduce David Wilkie?" said Paul Zetter, chairman of the Sports Aid Foundation at their London launching function. "What! You only won two medals in Montreal? Ernie could have done better than that . . ." as Eric Morecambe might have said (but didn't). (Courtesy of Sports Aid Foundation.)

Hardly competitive, but definitely decorative. Junketing in Jamaica. Playing the horses (from the left) I.T.V. personality Dickie Davies; Olympic modern pentathlon gold medallist Jim Fox; former world boxing champion John H. Stracey; David Wilkie, Britain's only individual champion in Montreal; and Alan Hime, President of the British Swimming Coaches' Association. The smiling riders, four of the finalists in the 1976 Speedo Miss Sports World contest, Christine Tranter, Annette Ramage, Sandra Hayes and (far right) Melanie Watt having a joke with David's girl friend Kate Kewley. (Photo: London Weekend Television)

On the left, former European heavyweight boxing champion Henry Cooper. On the right Ann Moore, Olympic show jumping silver medallist of 1972. And in the centre David Wilkie, with the medal presented by the Platinum Guild, in association with B.B.C. Television's Nationwide programme, for being the outstanding British male competitor at the Montreal Olympics. (Photo: Platinum Guild)

In America, you swim in various competitions and they are all neatly placed. The early ones, like the matches I had every two weeks for Miami, are to see how you are going. But the coaches don't expect their swimmers to be within a second of their best times all the time at this stage — something British coaches, often, do not understand. Now, I could do a 2 min. 6 sec. for 200 yards breaststroke three months before a big meet and be very pleased with it and so would my coach in the States. But if I told coaches over here what I had done, they would look at me and say 'that's six seconds off your best time.' They don't understand that it takes time to come down to get ready for the races that matter . . . they expect their swimmers to be ready all the time, to produce the goods all the time.

So the American winter programme leads up to the two big ones — the National Collegiate Athletic Association and the Amateur Athletic Union championships in late March and early April.

Take the N.C.A.A. This is the most exciting event in the world in which to take part and the standards are phenomenal. In an Olympics you only compete against three of America's best. In the N.C.A.A. you race against all of them!

Unfortunately, the N.C.A.A. is only open to teams from American universities and colleges. But if Britain competed in the A.A.U. meetings — the winter or summer ones (held usually in August) — which are the greatest national championships of all, I am sure it would improve all-over performances. It would give British swimmers the confidence that comes from the toughest competitive circuit in the world. It is a waste of time and money messing about at low level in Europe.

At the beginning, the Britons might be overawed by the occasion, just as I was at first. But after a couple of visits I'm damn sure they would get used to the pressures and prepare for them properly. And it would be far more valuable than going into a European meet where there may be only one or two swimmers in good racing form to beat. If you want to be a champion you have to have the chance to line up with seven other good people at one time and know you have to beat every single one of them as each one is capable of beating you. It should be this situation all the time — not just when the Olympics or World championships come along.

It amazes me that many coaches and officials over here would rather see our swimmers win medals from low-standard events rather than compete in high-level meetings and be beaten. The first is a kind of pot-hunting negative kind of approach because to lose in good company can be very positive! Some clubs do try to give their own swimmers this important chance to be among the best. But they have to raise the money themselves, they don't get any help from the people who have the cash . . . the swimming associations.

The American swimming system is like a pyramid with huge numbers of very good youngsters at the base, the numbers slowly reducing until you get real stars on the pinnacle. In Britain there is also a pyramid but there doesn't seem to be anything very much at the top.

There are many reasons for this, including the educational system . . . the fact that schools, colleges and universities don't do more . . . and the way the sport is administered.

Many British universities have their own pools, gymnasia etc., yet they don't make proper use of these. University swimming here is pretty well a joke. The people who do it look upon it more as a social scene, how much beer you can drink after the match. Certainly there's never been much importance placed on swimming at British universities.

Perhaps there are too many academics in this country who tend to look down upon sport . . . think it doesn't or shouldn't appeal to clever people. *But they are wrong.* To be healthy in body and mind is a true man or woman, but to have a healthy mind and a frail body is to be only half a person.

I don't think the colleges or universities in Britain produce as many great sports people as they should. *Something really has to be done about this. You are in the prime of your life when you are a student and you should be doing something more than just studying your life away.*

Maybe the powers that be in Britain haven't given any thought to this important aspect. The Amateur Swimming Association (of England) who have all the money seem to dominate everything in Britain and tell everyone what to do. This may be O.K. in some ways, but it is certainly bad in others, because people are not given a chance to express themselves.

The A.S.A. like swimmers who are nice and quiet and have no personalities . . . so they don't say anything against the establishment. And the A.S.A. can make people suffer — for they pick the teams and have absolute power over everybody, competitors, coaches and officials.

I think the problems in Britain are basic and changing the whole traditional set-up would be a tremendous job. I doubt whether the swimming associations as they are, would be prepared to do all the work involved and I don't think they would understand what it is all about anyway.

Worst of all, they are not prepared to listen to anybody who could tell them what it is all about. Their instant questions would be: 'what is it going to cost' and 'who is going to do it'.

They should seek the views of the people on the pool side, the swimmers and the coaches and believe that what they say is important. They should consider what all the other successful swimming nations in the world are doing to raise the standards of their competitors. And they should remember, even if Britain's men have had a good record at Olympic, World and European meetings recently, the success was achieved by a very few, many of whom were trained in the United States, and without any back-up reserves.

But the people in charge of British swimming, who collect a lot of money in the name of the sport, only want to spend the money the way they think and never how the people who really make up the sport think.

They could easily afford to pay the salaries of the top coaches in this country. After all England alone have assets of around £300,000, yet they were prepared to let Dave Haller lose £2,000 of his salary in 1976 for the privilege of coaching the British team for Montreal. *This is ridiculous.*

There are very few coaches in the whole world who are capable of getting a squad of swimmers — with their different personalities and abilities — on to the starting blocks ready for the big races. But I must be able, justifiably, to name one, and that is Haller. He has done this continuously and consistently for British teams for four years — from Belgrade and the World championships of 1973, Vienna and the European championships in 1974, the Cali, Colombia, World championships of 1975 and the 1976 Montreal Olympics.

The coach in charge of the final most important part of swimmers' preparations for something like the Olympics must have special qualities. For instance, that man is in charge of the taper and though some people may not think this is important *I can assure you that it is the most important part of the whole year's training and preparations.*

The coach has to bring the person down from a high plateau of work from which he is tired and not swimming very fast to the ideal state of not being tired and being capable of racing very quickly.

He isn't just concerned with the actual pool work, but also of preparing the competitors mentally for races. He must be a person in whom the swimmers have faith. In fact, a swimmer probably won't swim well if he doesn't have faith in the coach. It is very important to have someone there who understands you and whom you understand . . . to whom you can talk . . . who can relate to your own races and know you as an individual. And there are British coaches, even world coaches, who cannot handle this. They either give up, or try to train and prepare everyone the same way.

But Dave has a 'feel' for swimming. He has always been able to change according to the individual . . . he can be boisterous with some, or serious, quiet or intelligent with others. Yet I know his appointment has never been significant for some officials simply because they do not understand what we need. He has to be one of the best coaches in the world and the though of not choosing him, automatically, to be the British team coach is preposterous.

It isn't that Haller had done this just for me. It's the whole of the British men's team . . . Alan McClatchey, Gordon Downie, Brian Brinkley, Paul Naisby, Jimmy Carter, etc. etc. . . . and he has been mainly responsible for most of the big-time success of these people.

Don't forget that Haller was in charge of a squad of just eight men at the European championships in Vienna in 1974 and only one of the group didn't come back with at least one medal. In 1975, the British men's team of ten swimmers were named the B.B.C.'s "Sports Team of the Year" for coming second to the Americans at the World championships in Cali. And we were the fourth best men's team in Montreal, but of the eight men who reached finals, five were trained in America. Britain would have to look back almost to the turn of the century for such great success.

Yet at the time we were being assembled for the B.B.C. presentation, Dave was thinking seriously about resigning from his unpaid British coach's job. His club were forced to cut his salary because he would be spending nearly a third of the year in 1976 working for the British team and the swimming association officials would not agree to make it up for him.

I have used Dave Haller as an example of how it is in Britain. And with the right kind of encouragement and opportunities, I believe there could be more Hallers. But if the officials can treat a man like Dave in this way, what hope is there for younger and newer coaches on the way up, who have yet to prove themselves.

A coach has to be an artist in one sense of the word. He has to have a certain feel, to be able to manipulate swimmers as he would manipulate putty. He must know when to put on the pressure and work them hard, or have the courage to take them out of the water and rest them when they don't look good — as I had to rest before the World championships of 1975.

The establishment should understand that the coaches, from club level up, are the people who work for the sport. They must be in charge of the swimmers, as they are in America, and what they think is important. And they should not be ignored and insulted. They are the ones looking after the swimmers and it is they whose opinions are important. The coaches should be in charge, not a bunch of officials who seldom go on the pool-side and who don't know very much about swimming and swimmers, yet who make all the decisions.

Wouldn't it be nice if officials said 'How can we help you and your swimmers?' That is what should happen, that is the question which should be asked of the successful coaches who produce the swimmers who become our champions and make up our international teams. Of course, the swimming associations do spend money — but it is on their terms.

I once went to a training week at Crystal Palace where we did 100,000 metres in seven days. It was great, even if the aftermath was killing. But three weeks later, after everyone had gone back to their normal routines, it was as if the training week had never been.

I believe that the amateur associations are afraid that if they pay professionals to do professional jobs then they may find the amateurs — the timekeepers, judges and others who do so much of the work of the associations in organising swimming affairs — might want to be paid as well. But these are two totally different situations, one group are professionals and the other are amateurs. And it is very old fashioned to think that professionals do not have a vital and important part to play in amateur sport these days.

The establishment have got to get things into perspective. So a coach, or a team manager, doctor or physiotherapist, with a British swimming team should be entitled to be paid, or at least shouldn't be financially the poorer for doing a job that needs to be done.

I don't think the administration understand just how much it takes out of officials appointed to teams at, say, a World championships or Olympics. They put in a tremendous lot of effort, work from early in the morning to late at night, carry a lot of responsibility, suffer a lot of anxiety. So, the aim of the governing bodies of the sport should be to take the worries off the shoulders of the people working at pool-level. *It is a deplorable situation that this should not be understood and that it should be the way it is.*

There are many more coaches involved at high competitive level in the United States — full-time coaches and better paid than in Britain where so many are part-time. The American coaches have a status in the sport . . . and I only wish it was the same at home.

The competitive spirit, too, is much stronger and there is more pressure to win in America. At university level, coaches have pressure on them from their athletic departments and the alumni pressure the departments. In turn, the swimmers feel these combined pressures. I don't think it is a bad thing to work under the gun for to succeed in life you have to respond to pressure too.

More importance is placed on 'psyching up' in the States and this is probably explained by the differences in temperament between the U.S. and G.B. coaches. The Americans are more in tune with their swimmers and understand better what it takes to get a competitor motivated and excited for a race. They are able to relate at the swimmers' level.

Yet the rewards for competitors are not bigger and better in the U.S.A. than anywhere else. In fact, the only rewards from amateur sport are the satisfaction of your coaches, friends and yourself. And, in the long run, those are the only things that matter.

I shall never forget my time in Miami and I am indebted to the United States for giving me four years of fine education and successful swimming. It would be dishonest not to admit that, but it would be tremendous, in 1980 in Moscow, if another Briton could become an Olympic swimming champion and be able to say 'Thank you' — not to a foreign country but to his own.**"**

22

KATE

A bird's eye view

Away from the concentration of competition and the glamour of victory, the heartbreak of defeat and the crowded campus of the University of Miami, there is another David Wilkie. And since late 1973, where there is Wilkie there is Kate Kewley. Blonde Kate, slim and good-looking, is every Briton's idea of the all-American girl. Intelligent, too, with a degree in business administration from Purdue University at Lafayette, Indiana, and a Masters' degree in economics from Miami — of course — to prove it.

So, who better than Kate to talk about Wilkie the man . . . the swimmer away from the pool . . . perhaps the real David.

I think there are two sides to David — the public, smiling, cool, easy-to-get-along-with David and the private David. And even now, after three years, I don't understand him completely. He is a very private person.

We met in October 1973, a month or so after he had set his first world record, though I didn't know about that at the time. It was during my first semester. I'd only been at Miami a month and I was with a girl friend Sarah at the Rathskellar, the University beer hall. We saw David walking across the room and both said: 'That's a good-looking boy . . . like to meet him.' We just happened to bump into Greg Tye, who was on the swim squad, and without us saying anything he introduced us.

David was very quiet and we didn't say much . . . just hullo and how are you — that sort of thing. During the evening we ran into each other a few times — and more hullos. Then Sarah and I went back to our dorm. It had a tiny sitting room and two bedrooms which we shared with a couple of other girls. Greg and David went back to theirs, then they decided they would go for a walk. But they got as far as our rooms and never did go for that walk. Instead we sat talking until the wee small hours (a bit of Wilkie there).

As well as talking, we played chess and it was then that I learned something about David — though I didn't recognise it at the time. You see, even though I'm not much good at chess, I beat him and it was quite a blow to him. He couldn't believe that this unknown girl could beat him. So we had to play another game to prove he was better! Now, if we play darts, or bowls, billiards or pin-ball and I should happen to win, which isn't very often, we have to play another game to even the score.

I didn't realise then just how competitive he was. In fact, I didn't know anything about him. That, really, was the most unusual thing of all. David never mentioned he was a swimmer, that he had just come back from Belgrade having won a world title and set a world record . . . or that he was a silver medallist in Munich.

It was Greg who would say about David, 'Did you know this . . . do you know that . . .' David was never the one to say what he had done and it took me a few weeks to find about these things too. So I guess I got to know him as a regular person and not a sports star. I don't think he can ever doubt my reasons for liking him . . . because I honestly didn't know at the time. He was just a boy I met and liked.

What drew me to him the first night was that he was so quiet and interesting. We never ran out of things to say. That's what started our relationship for me.

At first I didn't even realise David was British. I thought he had a bit of an accent, maybe came from Boston. After three or four hours I said, 'You've got an accent', and he said, 'I'm Scottish'. That was the first shock.

The next was when I discovered I was two years older than David. He said he was 21. He'd added on two years and I never found out about it until weeks afterwards, when I just happened to be looking at his ID card and saw his birth date, 1954.

It wasn't until after Montreal that I learned about the background of his years at boarding school in Edinburgh. Spending so much time alone there and being away from his parents and everything, must have been a traumatic experience for him. And I think that explains a lot of how he is now.

David really does like to be alone . . . we can be together in my apartment (Kate moved into her own flat in December, 1974) and he will suddenly sit down in the living-room and put on headphones and listen to music for hours — by himself.

If we go out to the movies, we'll come back about 10, but instead of settling down together to watch TV or something, David will get his fishing gear together and go out fishing, until maybe two or three in the morning and leave me behind.

I don't go because he says he wants to be on his own . . . because he likes to think. I don't really know what he does out there by himself. But he did it quite frequently, and especially so in the two years leading up to Montreal.

I couldn't understand it at the beginning and it used to bother me a lot. I used to think 'why doesn't he want me to be around . . . what am I doing wrong?' I couldn't believe it was typical behaviour — it wasn't normal that we would be out for a few hours and he'd bring me home and then go off again by himself.

But gradually I began to see it wasn't me — that it was just the way David is. Now I understand it perfectly and it isn't a problem any more.

Since the Olympics in Montreal he's been leading a very public kind of life. People are always wanting him to do this, or that, come and do this and he is constantly busy. The time he has left he spilts up between us . . . but he has to get away by himself and think.

I think David is unique . . . to be the kind of person he is you have to be unique. To be a world-ranked competitor, to go through all that training, back and forth in the pool for hours every day as he did, you have to be a very strong person and in complete control of emotions and desires. David can do this.

David is very guarded about revealing his feelings, especially about personal matters. He doesn't want to reveal his deep thoughts, things that aren't related to swimming and I think that carries over into our relationship. He doesn't like any waves and if there are some he chooses to ignore them . . . just takes off.

He finds it difficult to come out of himself and talk about things. He is very reserved, holds back all the time. I think that goes back to his boarding school days . . . he didn't let himself go then and he still does that now to a certain degree. Maybe it is a self-protective thing or perhaps it is part of his mystique.

Now that did affect me early on. I used to get upset a lot because I didn't think he was making any attempt to understand me, or that he liked me . . . that he loved me. I felt rejected, but I gradually learned to accept the situation. Now I don't think it affects me any more. I'm used to the way he thinks and the things he does.

When we were both living on the campus we saw each other a lot because there really wasn't anywhere else for him to go. But that didn't mean everything went smoothly. He was touchy, moody, even bad-tempered at times, probably because he couldn't get away and could feel the tensions and pressures building up inside him before a big swim meet.

Later, in 1974, when I had an apartment and a car, he was able to go off on his fishing excursions and he was much easier to get along with. Then, when the N.C.A.A. or A.A.U. championships came along we didn't have the tensions we had in the past. He could get away from the university and the students and from me.

The discipline of training did affect him mentally — if not exhaust him mentally. It certainly did physically and it was a strain on our relationship. He wasn't in the mood for pleasantries then and it was very easy for me to get on his nerves. If I didn't cook the dinner right or talked too loudly he wouldn't have an all-out fight, he'd just take off on his own.

David doesn't like to admit he's wrong and if I tell him he is I really takes offence. He won't accept criticism from me. I think it is his way of expressing himself for when the coaches have criticised him and told him to go and do this or that, he was not in a position to argue.

If he knows people or he's with friends he will say if he doesn't like something, he will argue, have little tiffs . . . go through the whole range of emotions. He definitely has his own personality, but he is much more guarded when he is in public or with people he doesn't know very well.

What I am trying to put over is that in his relationships with the public, the press and so on, David comes across as 'a gentleman'. And he is a gentleman in every respect — but he's a real human person too.

He dislikes obnoxious situations, big parties and loud people. One thing that annoys him is that I talk too loudly — or at least he says I do. My voice rises above the crowd and he gets furious. He says, 'If you don't stop doing this I'll take you home.' The swim team sometimes had huge parties and even if we did go David wasn't the one to lead off the dancing. He'd get a beer and sit down with one or two people to talk.

Probably he would say Americans are loud and their humour is crude. But I think he has learned to like Americans and America. I think he would even consider living in the U.S. if the opportunities were there.

We like the movies and go to see everything we can, but very few we really like. David loved 'Jaws', but when he learned that the shark was a fake, a mechanical shark, he didn't want to go and we nearly didn't. He likes reality, and his favourite film was 'Blue Water White Death', about the search for a white shark. And he loves nature films and the television programme 'The Wild Kingdom'. David can watch these kind of things for hours and hours . . . they fascinate him.

Originally, when he came to Miami it was to study Marine Biology and he still has a big interest in this. He would have liked to continue but, because of the time he needed for his swimming, he moved over to Broadcasting and Communications, which gave him a more flexible timetable so that he could train too.

This course included photography and if he ever got the opportunity I think he would love to use this skill working under water . . . always, somehow, he comes back to the water. I hate to say he is a back-to-nature boy, but I guess that's what he is.

One of our hobbies is fish and I have two fish tanks in my apartment, one salt water and one fresh water. David completely stocked the salt water tank . . . going out in the ocean and catching little fish, crabs, snails, bringing back even the sand, stones and shells. And we had a baby lobster for a while, which he fed and nurtured, but it had to be put back in the ocean when it grew too big. He will turn on the lights over the tanks — and watch for hours as the fish swim round and round.

Whenever we have enough money to go out to eat, we go to Stone Crab Joe's on Miami Beach, to have the large stone crabs they serve there. It's ironic that all his interests come back to fish and water! Though he hasn't been too successful at fishing lately!

I think David's total catch from six months of fishing in 1976 was one six-inch fish!! Probably it was the only thing that defeated him that year — even if I admit that fishing off Miami shores is not that good.

When David is swimming in the pool he looks just like a huge whale — or maybe a shark is the right fish. And he comes at me — so fast — he just goes 'whoom'. There he comes, humming the theme song from 'Jaws' and he can be really frightening and I can't move quickly enough to get out of the pool.

I find it amazing to watch David in the water. I can sit and watch him all day, just going back and forth . . . not so much when he is practising but when he is playing. He's just like a fish, wiggling his body through the water, doing the weirdest movements. Other people would sink if they tried to do the things David can do.

He constantly plays in the water, diving to the bottom of the ocean and looking for little animals or shells. He always comes up with something. And if I'm not looking he will be ducking me in the water. He's just like a playful porpoise and I am sure he can swim as fast as a fish!!

With all his nervous energy, David is a prodigious eater and I cook for him quite a lot. He'll show up around 1 p.m. for breakfast just as I am thinking about dinner. And even since he gave up training he's still a great food man. He says his appetite has gone down since Montreal but I haven't noticed it one bit.

His breakfast usually consists of three eggs, five sausages, two pieces of toast with jelly (jam in English) and peanut butter *together*, a bowl of cereal (usually rice crispies), some juice and a huge milk shake full of all kinds of nutritious things.

Dinner? He eats a normal one, except that he has three piled-high helpings. He's a meat and potatoes type and the one other vegetable he likes is peas, and he'll have these nine times out of ten.

One of his favourite meals is stoveys — a kind of stew and he cooks it much better than me. Usually he makes it with liver, potatoes and onions. Then he likes — or would like — to have suet dishes, but we don't seem to have the right ingredients in the States for David has tried to make this a few times, unsuccessfully.

The most unsuccessful cooking experiment has been trying to make a fudge like sweet (David calls it tablet) which his father used to make in Ceylon. It's like soft candy, seems to take pounds of sugar, quarts of milk, and condensed milk. We cook and stir and stir and cook yet never seem to get the right temperature. It has never come out right and we've had pans and pans of this candy lying all round the apartment — horrible — and eventually I have to scrape it out and throw it away.

To this day David has never actually gotten the recipe, even though he could have written it down when he saw his family. And he still keeps trying. David thinks himself as quite a cook and loves to do it . . . just throwing things together. He is quite proud of his accomplishments — although, at times, it's . . . ugh!

I was surprised he could eat so much . . . and a little bit jealous too. He's so thin, slim hipped, flat stomached and I'm having to watch the calories while he's putting down so much food.

Since he has quit his regular work-outs, his intake of food has cut down a bit and he has put on a little weight. I can see it round his middle. I kid him a bit about that, saying he is getting out of shape, but David doesn't like that one bit. He'll say, 'I don't think that at all' — then check on the scales. But one day he weighed and found he had put on a bit and was slightly taken aback. He gave up his milk shake that day!

Three years is a long time to carry on a relationship, especially considering the fact that David has been constantly on the go and travelling. He has been round the world several times since I have known him so we are as many months apart as we are together.

I don't think it was easy for David to have a relationship with a girl that lasted a long time. There must be a feeling of responsibility after a while and that is something David has been fighting constantly. He has so many things on his mind — swimming, studies, family across the ocean — so I was just another tie and I think he was afraid of that, of committing himself, of any relationship being for all time, for ever.

So what happened was that we were not involved and then, all of a sudden, we were involved and there was not much he could do about it then, except accept the situation. But he fights against it at times.

At the beginning I couldn't understand, but I realise now that he likes and needs his freedom. To David, marriage looks something like a prison, where he would cease to be his own man. But I think he is changing.

I wouldn't want him to be a 9-5 person and I think that is why we have got along so well. When he goes away on his trips, of course I am sad to see him go . . . but it's always so nice when he comes back. It keeps a little zest in our relationship. Certainly when we started out in 1973, we had no idea that we would be together even three years from then, for David had a lot of growing to do and a lot of places to go.''

23

WILKIE ABOUT WILKIE

Me on me

'' For all those who have seen me or read about me, liked me or hated me, met me and shaken my hand or wondered who the hell I was . . . this is David Wilkie.

Swimming has forced me into the public eye, to become public orientated . . . forced me to realise that people want to know about me, how Wilkie works, how Wilkie ticks, how Wilkie talks. This was something I had always wanted to escape in my life. I like to do things on my own and I've never liked to be part of a large group. This doesn't mean that I don't like people's company. I do. And I like most people — though there are a few I just can't stand . . . those who try to make out they are something that they really are not.

They are the people who think they have to impress me with their behaviour, because they think I am different . . . or think I am so big-headed they have to make out they are just as good as me. There is no need for that.

I've always been quiet about my successes — that's not to say I don't enjoy them, but I'd rather have people find out than for me to tell them. I don't think anyone can say I'm big-headed. I treat my successes rather coolly, though I am very proud to have achieved what I have achieved. I'd rather walk down the street and not be noticed than be noticed.

Over the years I have made silly mistakes . . . like that 100 metres stupidity in the European championships in Vienna . . . the time I crashed my head against the pool-end during the 200 metres medley final at the Belgrade World championships . . . and when I didn't qualify for the medley final at the Cali World championships. Anyway, they prove I'm a human being and not infallible.

I always like to win races, yet when I lost the 100 metres breast-stroke in Montreal I wasn't broken-hearted. But I expected so much of myself in the 200 metres . . . if I had lost that one it would have been a different story because I had trained for that race for a long time and I thought I was capable of winning.

Defeat would have been a very hard thing for me to accept, for nothing before, not even the World championships, was ever as important as that one race in Montreal. It was my great moment . . . the most important part of my life because it gave me strength and a greater belief in myself. I had always thought I was capable of doing something and being able to prove it to myself, even in a small way like that: that I had done the right thing, in training and preparation and competed against the best in the world, is something to look back on with tremendous pleasure.

I see my life clearly in three stages:

Ceylon — where I was a boisterous young lad and seemed to get on very well with people and wasn't a bit shy . . .

Edinburgh — where I changed a lot at school, became very self-centered, shy with people I didn't know, wouldn't speak to people I didn't know and made no attempt to communicate, even with people I did know . . .

Miami — where I grew up and found myself.

Because of the changes I went through, I suppose I became very independent, having fended for myself from a young age and I knew what I wanted. If I didn't want to do something, I got it into my head that I didn't have to do it. I think this is why, during my Edinburgh days, if I didn't want to swim I didn't see why I should.

When you are young, you don't see that you have a big future ahead of you, because you only think about the present time.

Boarding schools can be good in some ways and bad in others. They separate you from your family and friends. But I think that the independence I learned at boarding school, being in charge of myself and making my own decisions when I was quite young, led later to being able to fend for myself and not participate in group actions quite so much.

Certainly it prepared me for my four years in America. A lot of people who go to the United States get homesick in their first year. But I was used to being away from home and used to having to make new friends all the time, so I was lucky.

Swimming makes people very competitive . . . you have to be if you are to challenge everyone else. And it also reflects on everything else you do. I think I have become a much more competitive person since I went to America; they breed that into you there for the whole way of life is very competitive, not just in sport but everything. Now I think it is lucky for me and my life that I have this determination to do well — which comes from swimming.

It would be a lie if I said I didn't enjoy reading what people write about me. But it does annoy me when things are written the wrong way. It gets me very annoyed, in fact, for people get the wrong impression. The thing I hate most is being misquoted because what is published, what the media say, does influence people and you can be made to look a fool.

When I landed back from Montreal, reporters asked me about the conditions at the Olympics and I made a remark that some of the athletes weren't too pleased with the village. The press boys laughed but then, in the papers, the headlines said: 'Wilkie slams athletes. That really got me quite annoyed, but there was nothing I could do about it. The damage had been done.

I suppose every swimmer likes publicity, but it does get to be a bit of an embarrassment if you get it all and no one else gets any. You find everybody wants to know a winner and always the guy who comes in second is forgotten. These are the facts of life, but it's a shame it has to be like that. Everybody who competes at Olympic level really is a winner.

I remember being interviewed in Scotland when I had beaten my great friend Gordon Stirton, who was my early swimming inspiration, for the first time. Gordon was there and afterwards he said 'They are only interested in you when you win, but when you are back they don't care about you.' And that's true, because they didn't care about Gordon any more after I had taken over as Scotland's top breaststroke swimmer. Once someone beats you, they get all the attention. But that's the way of the world.

I have been very lucky, too, with swimming. It has opened up a lot of doors and given me a good future. I have been offered many opportunities which wouldn't have come if I hadn't won in Montreal. So my gold medal has been fortunate for me in that respect.

The good thing about having a university degree is that if things don't work out, at least there is something to fall back on — even though I don't expect to use my degree in broadcasting and communications for a few years yet. Maybe, if the degree doesn't count

The perfect pair. British Olympic 200 metres breaststroke champions. Anita Lonsbrough, winner in Rome in 1960, presents David Wilkie with the "Sportsman of the Month" award at London's Sportsman Club, to honour his victory in Montreal in 1976. (Photo: Daily Mirror)

Aberdeen — a chubby David full of Christm͏as
fare, in 1958 and, 18 years later, celebrating
Montreal Olympics victories with Caroline a͏nd
Jean Wilkie. (Courtesy Wilkie family.)

for much in Great Britain, I would be prepared to return to America, but I don't want to do that.

Right now I think it is important for me to come back to Britain. I'd like to return to my family and to get back into the British way of life again. I've spent 11 years in Ceylon, six in Britain and four in the United States. Yet I am British at heart and Britain is my home.''

David Wilkie is a realist. He has said so, without hedging or subterfuge in this book, judged his own actions and reactions and talked about them as frankly as he has done about those of the other people in his life.

Perhaps the most realistic statement he has ever made came within a month of his Montreal Olympics triumph. "People don't remember a gold medallist for that long. They quickly begin to look for the next one . . . and the one after that."

Sweeping generalisations of that kind may be true or not and certainly they are open to argument. Equally certain is that David Wilkie, the independent man, who accepts happily yet modestly the glory of his own achievements, will be around in memories longer than he thinks.

24

VITAL STATISTICS

ABBREVIATIONS

AUS	Australia	IRE	Ireland
AUT	Austria	IRN	Iran
BEL	Belgium	ISL	Iceland
BRA	Brazil	ITA	Italy
BUL	Bulgaria	JPN	Japan
CAN	Canada	MEX	Mexico
DEN	Denmark	NIR	Northern Ireland
ECU	Ecuador	NOR	Norway
ENG	England	NZL	New Zealand
ESP	Spain	PER	Peru
FIJ	Fiji	PNG	Papua and New Guinea
FIN	Finland	POL	Poland
FRA	France	PUR	Puerto Rico
GBR	Great Britain	SCO	Scotland
GDR	German Democratic Republic (East)	SWE	Sweden
		TCH	Czechoslovakia
GER	German Federal Republic (West)	TUR	Turkey
		URS	Soviet Union
GRE	Greece	USA	United States
HKG	Hong Kong	VEN	Venezuela
HOL	Netherlands	WAL	Wales
HUN	Hungary	YUG	Yugoslavia

Short-course = Pools shorter than 50 metres.
Long-course = Pools of 50 metres or 55 yards.
A.A.U. = Amateur Athletic Union (of the USA).
N.C.A.A. = National Collegiate Athletic Association.

MEDALS

OLYMPIC

1972 Munich	200 metres breaststroke	Silver	2.23.67 e/c
1976 Montreal	100 metres breaststroke	Silver	1:03.43 e/c
	200 metres breaststroke	Gold	2:15.11 w/e/c

WORLD

1973 Belgrade	200 metres breaststroke	Gold	2:19.28 w/e/c
	200 metres medley	Bronze	2:08.84 c
1975 Cali	100 metres breaststroke	Gold	1:04.26 e/c
	200 metres breaststroke	Gold	2:18.23 e/c
	4 × 100 metres medley	Bronze	3:52.80
	(*Jimmy Carter, David Wilkie, Brian Brinkley, Gordon Downie*)		

EUROPEAN

1974 Vienna	200 metres breaststroke	Gold	2:20.42
	200 metres medley	Gold	2:06.32 w/e/c
	4 × 100 metres medley	Silver	3:54.13
	(*Colin Cunningham, David Wilkie, Steve Nash, Brian Brinkley*)		

COMMONWEALTH

1970 Edinburgh	200 metres breaststroke	Bronze	2:32.87
1974 Christchurch	100 metres breaststroke	Silver	1:07.37
	200 metres breaststroke	Gold	2:24.42
	200 metres medley	Gold	2:10.11

RECORDS

WORLD

200 metres breaststroke	Belgrade	6 September, 1973	2:19.28
	Montreal	24 July, 1976	2:15.11
200 metres medley	Vienna	24 August, 1974	2:06.32

EUROPEAN

100 metres breaststroke	Cali	22 July, 1975	1:04.26
	Montreal	20 July, 1976	1:03.43
200 metres breaststroke	Munich	2 September, 1972	2:23.67
	Belgrade	6 September, 1973	2:20.94
	Belgrade	6 September, 1973	2:19.28
	Cali	24 July, 1975	2:18.23
	Montreal	24 July, 1976	2:15.11
200 metres medley	Vienna	24 August, 1974	2:06.32
	Long Beach	4 April, 1976	2:06.25

COMMONWEALTH

100 metres breaststroke	Munich	29 August, 1972	1:06.35
	Munich	29 August, 1972	1:06.25
	Belgrade	4 September, 1973	1:05.74
	Prague	5 April, 1975	1:05.7* eq
	Cali	22 July, 1975	1:04.26
	Montreal	20 July, 1976	1:03.43
200 metres breaststroke	Edinburgh	29 July, 1972	2:26.76
	Munich	2 September, 1972	2:24.54
	Munich	2 September, 1972	2:23.67
	Belgrade	6 September, 1973	2:20.94
	Belgrade	6 September, 1973	2:19.28
	Cali	24 July, 1975	2:18.23
	Montreal	24 July, 1976	2:15.11
200 metres medley	London	23 April, 1973	2:10.0*
	Belgrade	7 September, 1973	2:09.61
	Belgrade	7 September, 1973	2:08.84
	Vienna	24 August, 1974	2:08.48
	Vienna	24 August, 1974	2:06.32
	Long Beach	4 April, 1976	2:06.25

w = World record.   e = European record.

c = Commonwealth record.   eq = record equalled.

* = time taken to tenths of a second.

WILKIE'S BEST OF THE YEAR

Year	100 metres Breaststroke	200 metres Breaststroke	200 metres Medley
1969	(np) 1:20.6* East Kilbride	(np) 2:51.9* East Kilbride	
1970	(np) 1:10.8* Edinburgh	(35) 2:32.54 Edinburgh	(np) 2:25.6* Edinburgh
1971	(np) 1:10.5* Edmonton	(44) 2:32.6* Edmonton	(np) 2:21.4* Edmonton
1972	(9) 1:06.25c Munich	(4) 2:23.67ec Munich	(21) 2:12.4* London
1973	(4) 1:05.74 Belgrade	(1) 2:19.28wec Belgrade	(4) 2:08.84 Belgrade
1974	(13) 1:06.96 Blackpool	(2) 2:20.42 Vienna	(1) 2:06.32wec Vienna
1975	(1) 1:04.26ec Cali	(1) 2:18.23ec Cali	(11) 2:09.29 Moscow
1976	(2) 1:03.43ec Montreal	(1) 2:15.11wec Montreal	(1) 2:06.25ec Long Beach

w = World record *e = European record* *c = Commonwealth record*

Figure in brackets = World ranking position of the year   (np) = not placed in year

* = Time taken to tenths

WILKIE'S PROGRESS
(long-course, 50 metre or 55 yard pool performance only)

w = World record   or = Olympic record   e = European record

c = Commonwealth record   ch = Championships record   b = British record

sc = Scottish record

h = heat time   sf = semi-final time   f = final time

y = yards distance (ie 110 or 220 yards)

Figure in brackets (1) = position against the total entry in heats, semi-finals or final. If there is no figure in brackets it indicates that the event was a match or an event decided on time classification.

100 metres breaststroke

1969

Scottish championships (junior)	East Kilbride	July 15	f	1:20.6y	(2)

1970

British trials	Crystal Palace	March 14		1:13.4y	(3)
Multi-nation meeting	Blackpool	May 15/16	f	1:14.7y	(4)
Iceland v. Scotland	Reykjavik	June 12/13		1:13.0	(2)
Scotland v. Denmark	Edinburgh	July 6		1:10.8	(1) sc
Commonwealth Games	Edinburgh	July 20	h	1:11.4	(5)
		July 21	f	1:11.0	(5)
European championships	Barcelona	September 5	h	1:12.4	(18)
Scottish championships	Edinburgh	September 26	f	1:13.36	(1)

1971

Canadian championships	Edmonton, Alb	July 8/11	f	1:10.5	(3) sc

1972

Britain v. Holland	Crystal Palace	March 3/4		1:11.1	(1)
West German International	West Berlin	April 7	h	1:11.80	(14)
		April 8	sf	1:11.20	(10)
Olympic time trial	Leeds	May 28		1:10.0	(1) sc
Scottish championships	Edinburgh	June 9	f	1:10.4	(1)
National championships/ Olympic trials	Crystal Palace	July 14	f	1:08.3	(2) sc
Olympic Games	Munich	August 29	h	1:06.35	(5) c
		August 29	sf	1:06.25	(8) c
		August 30	f	1:06.52	(8)

1973

South African Games	Pretoria	March 29/31	f	1:08.8	(1)
Five-Nations	Dortmund	April 14/15		1:07.9	(2)
Coca-Cola International	Crystal Palace	April 21/22		1:06.3	(1)
Santa Clara International	Santa Clara	June 22/24	f	1:08.93	(5)

0 metres breaststroke continued

ational championships	Coventry	August 3	h	1:08.79	(3)
		August 3	f	1:07.88	(1)
uropa Cup	East Berlin	August 19		1:07.1	(3)
orld championships	Belgrade	September 6	h	1:06.98	(6)
		September 6	f	1:05.74	(4) c/b

74

ommonwealth Games	Christchurch	January 31	h	1:07.78	(1) ch
		February 1	f	1:07.37	(2)
ational championships	Blackpool	July 19	h	1:08.3	(1)
		July 19	f	1:06.96	(1)
uropean championships	Vienna	August 19	h	*1:14.79	(23)

After stopping for about 8 sec. mid-race thinking there had been a false start

75

zechoslovakia v. Scotland v. Hungary	Prague	April 5		1:05.7	(1) c/b eq.
orld championships	Cali	July 22	h	1:06.40	(6)
		July 22	f	1:04.26	(1) c/c/b
uropa Cup	Moscow	August 16		1:05.49	(1) ch

76

AU (US) championships	Long Beach	April 1	h	1:05.42	(3)
		April 1	f	1:04.46	(1)
lympic Games	Montreal	July 19	h	1:05.19	(5)
		July 19	sf	1:04.29	(4)
		July 20	f	1:03.43	(2) c/c/b

---

00 metres breaststroke

969

cottish championships (junior)	East Kilbride	July 20	f	2:57.9y	(3)

970

ritish trials	Crystal Palace	March 14		2:42.7y	(3) sc
ritain v. Soviet Union	Edinburgh	April 24		2:39.7	(3) sc
cottish trials	Edinburgh	May		2:39.9	(1)
leven-nations	Blackpool	May 15/16		2:40.8	(2)
celand v. Scotland	Reykjavik	June 12/13		2:38.1	(2) sc
ritain v. Holland (junior)	Crystal Palace	June 19/20		2:36.8y	(1) sc
cotland v. Denmark	Edinburgh	July 7		2:32.9	(1) b
ommonwealth Games	Edinburgh	July 17	h	2:32.54	(2) b
		July 18	f	2:32.87	(3)
uropean championships	Barcelona	September 9	h	2:40.0	(20)
cottish championships	Edinburgh	September 23	f	2:39.44	(1)

200 metres breaststroke continued

1971

Canadian championships	Edmonton, Alb.	July 8/11	f	2:32.6	(1)

1972

Britain v. Holland	Crystal Palace	March 3/4		2:34.5	(2)
West German	West Berlin	April 8	h	2:32.26	(1) b
International		April 9	f	2:30.96	(2) b
Scottish championships	Edinburgh	June 10	h	2:32.1	(1)
		June 10	f	2:38.4	(1)
National championships/	Crystal Palace	July 15		2:28.0	(1) b
Olympic trials					
Eight-nations	Edinburgh	July 29		2:26.76	(1) c/b
Olympic Games	Munich	September 2	h	2:24:54	(2) c/b
		September 2	f	2:23.67	(2) e/c/b

1973

South African Games	Pretoria	March 29/31	f	2:30.2	(1)
Five-Nations	Dortmund	April 14/15		2:27.5	(1)
Coca-Cola International	Crystal Palace	April 21/22		2:23.8	(1)
Santa Clara International	Santa Clara	June 22/24	f	2:27.0	(1)
National championships	Coventry	August 4	h	2:33.38	(1)
		August 4	f	2:27.60	(1)
Scottish championships	Edinburgh	August 16	f	2:29.54	(1)
Europa Cup	East Berlin	August 20		2:26.09	(3)
World championships	Belgrade	September 6	h	2:20.94	(1) e/c/b
		September 6	f	2:19.28	(1) w/e/c

1974

Commonwealth Games	Christchurch	January 26	h	2:30.79	(6)
		January 30	f	2:24.42	(1) ch
National championships	Blackpool	July 20	h	2:31.4	(1)
		July 20	f	2:26.3	(1)
European championships	Vienna	August 23	h	2:24.37	(2)
		August 23	f	2:20.42	(1) ch

1975

British World	Crystal Palace	May 24		2:26.28	(1)
championships trials					
World championships	Cali	July 24	h	2:21.90	(1)
		July 24	f	2:18.23	(1) e/c/b/c
Europa Cup	Moscow	August 17		2:20.93	(1) ch

1976

AAU (US) championships	Long Beach	April 3	h	2:21.73	(1)
		April 3	f	2:18.48	(1)
Olympic Games	Montreal	July 24	h	2:18.29	(1) or
		July 24	f	2:15.11	(1) w/or/c

etres medley

nonwealth Games	Edinburgh	July 20	h	2:25.6	(10)
sh championships	Edinburgh	September 26	f	2:32.46	(1)
ior)					
lian championships	Edmonton, Alb.	July 8/11	h	2:21.4	(np) sc
German	West Berlin	April 7	h	2:18.61	(7) sc
rnational		April 8	f	2:21.42	(8)
pic time trials	Leeds	May 28		2:20.2	(1)
sh championships	Edinburgh	June 9	f	2:15.3	(1) sc
nal championships/	Crystal Palace	July 13	f	2:12.4	(2) sc
mpic trials					
pic Games	Munich	September 3	h	2:13.25	(12)
Cola International	Crystal Palace	April 23		2:10.0	(2) b
nal championships	Coventry	August 2	f	2:12.96	(2)
championships	Belgrade	September 7	h	2:09.61	(2) c/b
		September 7	f	2:08.84	(3) c/b
nonwealth Games	Christchurch	January 28	h	2:14.39	(2)
		January 30	f	2:10.11	(1) ch
nal championships	Blackpool	July 19	f	2:12.3	(1)
ean championships	Vienna	August 24	h	2:08.48	(1) c/b
		August 24	f	2:06.32	(1) w/ch/e/c/b
n World	Crystal Palace	May 25		2:13.04	(1)
mpionships trials					
championships	Cali	July 25	h	2:12.68	(9)
a Cup	Moscow	August 16		2:09.29	(1) ch
(US) championships	Long Beach	April 4	h	2:08.56	(3)
		April 4	f	2:06.25	(1) e/c/b
a Cup	Pescara	August 14		2:09.06	(2)

OLYMPIC GAMES — MUNICH

29. aug   12:12   schwimmhalle olympiapark
schwimmen   swimming
100 m brust herren   100 m breaststroke men
ergebnis   result
vorlaeufe---------------------- heats--------------------

	name		50m	100m	qua.
1.	chatfield, mark	usa	30, 73	1 : 05, 89	*
2.	hencken, john	usa	31, 02	1 : 05, 96	*
3.	taguchi, nobutaka	jpn	31, 53	1 : 06, 07	*
4.	fiolo, jose sylvio	bra	31, 62	1 : 06, 23	*
5.	wilkie, david	gbr	31, 26	1 : 06, 35	*
6.	bruce, tom	usa	31, 49	1 : 06, 45	*
7.	kusch, walter	ger	32, 50	1 : 06, 95	*
8.	mahony, william	can	31, 94	1 : 07, 14	*
9.	pankin, nikolai	urs	31, 08	1 : 07, 31	*
10.	katzur, klaus	gdr	31, 68	1 : 07, 36	*
11.	kosinskiy, vladimir	urs	31, 94	1 : 07, 39	*
12.	combet, bernard	fra	31, 69	1 : 08, 08	*
13.	stulikov, viktor	urs	31, 63	1 : 08, 18	*
14.	stoddart, robert	can	31, 99	1 : 08, 44	*
15.	menu, roger	fra	32, 09	1 : 08, 63	*
16.	hradetzky, rainer	gdr	31, 98	1 : 08, 67	*
17.	whittaker, michael	can	32, 22	1 : 08, 86	
18.	guenther, michael	ger	32, 55	1 : 08, 93	
19.	munoz, k felipe	mex	32, 35	1 : 08, 95	
20.	jarvie, paul	aus	32, 66	1 : 09, 26	
21.	jalmaani, amman	phi	32, 56	1 : 09, 28	
22.	oconnell, malcolm	gbr	32, 00	1 : 09, 33	
23.	balcells, pedro	esp	32, 87	1 : 09, 37	
24.	boretto, armando osvaldo	arg	31, 42	1 : 09, 64	
25.	ball, liam	irl	32, 81	1 : 09, 68	
	szabo, sandor	hun	32, 35	1 : 09, 68	
27.	kriechbaum, steffen	aut	32, 67	1 : 09, 87	
28.	toth, janos	hun	32, 68	1 : 10, 02	
29.	hellmann, andreas	ger	32, 46	1 : 10, 13	
30.	salcedo, gustavo	mex	31, 92	1 : 10, 17	
31.	dubey, jean pierre	sui	33, 04	1 : 10, 31	
32.	tchakarov, anghel	bul	32, 56	1 : 10, 34	
33.	smiglak, cezary	pol	32, 93	1 : 10, 53	
34.	sokhon, yi	khm	32, 36	1 : 11, 00	
35.	naisby, paul	gbr	32, 77	1 : 11, 05	
36.	gudmundsson, gudjon	isl	32, 76	1 : 11, 11	
37.	koch, karl chr	den	33, 64	1 : 11, 27	
38.	hunger, alfredo	per	34, 06	1 : 11, 44	
39.	mingione, edmondo	ita	32, 93	1 : 11, 75	
40.	koutoumanis, theodoros	gre	33, 96	1 : 12, 05	
41.	vingherhoets, rudi	bel	34, 69	1 : 12, 59	
42.	faruk, morkal	tur	33, 63	1 : 13, 86	
43.	ferracuti, piero	sal	35, 18	1 : 16, 74	
44.	bassoul, bruno	lib	36, 63	1 : 19, 94	
	aguerrevere, antonio	ven		na	

29. aug   17:36   schwimmhalle olympiapark
chwimmen   swimming
00 m brust herren   100 m breaststroke men
rgebnis   result
wischenlauf 1-------------------- semi-final 1----------------

	name		50m	100m
.	hencken, john	usa	31, 14	1:05, 68 nwr
2.	fiolo, jose sylvio	bra	31, 30	1:05, 99
3.	bruce, tom	usa	31, 40	1:06, 05
4.	katzur, klaus	gdr	32, 65	1:06, 82
5.	mahony, william	can	31, 70	1:07, 06
6.	combet, bernard	fra	31, 80	1:07, 76
7.	stoddart, robert	can	32, 31	1:08, 61
8.	hradetzky, rainer	gdr	32, 73	1:09, 49

29. aug   17:45   schwimmhalle olympiapark
schwimmen   swimming
00 m brust herren   100 m breaststroke men
ergebnis   result
zwischenlauf 2-------------------- semi-final 2----------------

	name		50m	100m
1.	taguchi, nobutaka	jpn	31, 27	1:05, 13 nwr
2.	kusch, walter	ger	31, 41	1:05, 78
3.	pankin, nikolai	urs	31, 92	1:06, 08
4.	chatfield, mark	usa	30, 76	1:06, 08
5.	wilkie, david	gbr	31, 55	1:06, 25
6.	stulikov, viktor	urs	31, 83	1:06, 66
7.	kosinskiy, vladimir	urs	31, 53	1:07, 08
8.	menu, roger	fra	30, 81	1:07, 75

wr   1:05, 7
or   1:05, 7

29. aug 17:56   schwimmhalle olympiapark
schwimmen   swimming
100 m brust herren   100 m breaststroke men
ergebnis   result
zwischenlaeufe------------------- semi-finals---------------

	name		50m	100m	qual
1.	taguchi, nobutaka	jpn	31, 27	1:05, 13	*
2.	hencken, john	usa	31, 14	1:05, 68	*
3.	kusch, walter	ger	31, 41	1:05, 78	*
4.	fiolo, jose sylvio	bra	31, 30	1:05, 99	*
5.	bruce, tom	usa	31, 40	1:06, 05	*
6.	pankin, nikolai	urs	31, 92	1:06, 08	*
	chatfield, mark	usa	30, 76	1:06, 08	*
8.	wilkie, david	gbr	31, 55	1:06, 25	*
9.	stulikov, viktor	urs	31, 83	1:06, 66	
10.	katzur, klaus	gdr	32, 65	1:06, 82	
11.	mahony, william	can	31, 70	1:07, 06	
12.	kosinskiy, vladimir	urs	31, 53	1:07, 08	
13.	menu, roger	fra	30, 81	1:07, 75	
14.	combet, bernard	fra	31, 80	1:07, 76	
15.	stoddart, robert	can	32, 31	1:08, 61	
16.	hradetzky, rainer	gdr	32, 73	1:09, 49	

30. aug 18:47   schwimmhalle olympiapark
schwimmen   swimming
100 m brust herren   100 m breaststroke men
ergebnis   result
endlauf------------------------- final---------------------

	name		50m	100m	
1.	taguchi, nobutaka	jpn	31, 38	1:04, 94	nw
2.	bruce, tom	usa	30, 66	1:05, 43	
3.	hencken, john	usa	30, 74	1:05, 61	
4.	chatfield, mark	usa	30, 81	1:06, 01	
5.	kusch, walter	ger	31, 46	1:06, 23	
6.	fiolo, jose sylvio	bra	31, 03	1:06, 24	
7.	pankin, nikolai	urs	31, 27	1:06, 36	
8.	wilkie, david	gbr	31, 02	1:06, 52	

wr   1:05, 1
or   1:05, 1

schwimmen / swimming / natation
200 m brust herren / 200 m breaststroke men / 200 m brasse hommes
ergebnis / result / resultat
vorlaeufe — heats — series

	name		50m	100m	150m	200m	qual
1.	taguchi, nobutaka	jpn	33,23	1:09,59	1:46,57	2:23,45	*
2.	wilkie, david	gbr	33,92	1:12,10	1:47,87	2:24,54	*
3.	hencken, john	usa	32,52	1:09,63	1:47,08	2:24,88	*
4.	colella, rick	usa	33,79	1:11,27	1:47,74	2:25,40	*
5.	munoz, k felipe	mex	34,52	1:12,04	1:49,06	2:25,99	*
6.	cherdakov, igor	urs	33,04	1:11,21	1:48,38	2:26,21	*
7.	katzur, klaus	gdr	32,75	1:10,26	1:48,51	2:26,32	*
8.	kusch, walter	ger	34,11	1:12,52	1:49,41	2:26,43	*
9.	pankin, nikolai	urs	33,38	1:10,45	1:47,95	2:26,71	
	mahony, william	can	33,40	1:11,41	1:48,97	2:26,71	
11.	job, brian	usa	33,98	1:11,54	1:48,80	2:26,91	
12.	jarvie, paul	aus	33,94	1:11,68	1:49,55	2:27,83	
13.	kosinskiy, vladimir	urs	33,77	1:11,47	1:49,15	2:28,00	
14.	balcells, pedro	esp	34,79	1:13,58	1:51,14	2:29,29	
15.	menu, roger	fra	33,14	1:11,30	1:50,37	2:30,05	
16.	stoddart, robert	can	34,25	1:12,12	1:50,42	2:30,08	
17.	kriechbaum, steffen	aut	32,99	1:11,76	1:49,84	2:30,09	
18.	fiolo, jose sylvio	bra	33,54	1:11,20	1:50,10	2:30,21	
19.	tchakarov, anghel	bul	34,87	1:12,34	1:51,18	2:30,27	
20.	oconnell, malcolm	gbr	33,41	1:12,73	1:51,40	2:31,21	
21.	dubey, jean pierre	sui	34,51	1:12,60	1:52,00	2:31,56	
22.	gudmundsson, gudjon	isl	34,52	1:13,35	1:52,85	2:32,40	
23.	hradetzky, rainer	gdr	34,32	1:13,40	1:52,50	2:32,48	
24.	hellmann, andreas	ger	33,61	1:12,66	1:51,83	2:32,60	
25.	salcedo, gustavo	mex	34,45	1:13,48	1:52,75	2:32,81	
26.	ball, liam	irl	35,62	1:14,13	1:53,21	2:33,47	
	whittaker, michael	can	33,96	1:13,49	1:53,34	2:33,47	
28.	jalmaani, amman	phi	34,43	1:13,70	1:53,60	2:33,54	

200m breaststroke men continued over

200m breaststroke men continued

			50m	100m	150m	200m
29.	johnson, nigel	gbr	34,47	1:12,30	1:52,11	2:34,37
30.	smiglak, cezary	pol	34,03	1:13,42	1:52,95	2:34,51
31.	sokhon, yi	khm	34,13	1:13,68	1:53,54	2:34,77
32.	di pietro, michele	ita	35,00	1:14,33	1:55,55	2:36,49
33.	vingherhoets, rudi	bel	35,07	1:14,61	1:55,58	2:36,89
34.	betz, gregor	ger	34,42	1:14,19	1:54,92	2:36,96
35.	hunger, alfredo	per	34,53	1:14,63	1:55,77	2:37,20
36.	toth, janos	hun	34,74	1:14,51	1:56,11	2:37,40
37.	koch, karl chr	den	35,30	1:15,44	1:55,95	2:38,47
38.	faruk, morkal	tur	37,18	1:18,90	2:01,52	2:43,69
39.	ferracuti, piero	sal	36,14	1:18,54	2:03,02	2:45,73
40.	cabrera, alejandro	sal	38,52	1:22,53	2:09,34	2:56,60
	aguerrevere, antonio	ven				na
	boretto, armando osvaldo	arg				dq
	koutoumanis, theodoros	gre				na

2. sept 18:41　schwimmhalle olympiapark

schwimmen / swimming
natation
200 m brust herren / 200 m breaststroke men / 200 m brasse hommes
ergebnis / result / resultat
endlauf / final / finale

	name		50m	100m	150m	200m
1.	hencken, john	usa	31,55	1:08,34	1:45,35	2:21,55 nwr
2.	wilkie, david	gbr	33,45	1:11,37	1:47,41	2:23,67
3.	taguchi, nobutaka	jpn	32,93	1:10,87	1:47,61	2:23,88
4.	colella, rick	usa	33,49	1:10,31	1:47,17	2:24,28
5.	munoz, k felipe	mex	34,09	1:11,72	1:49,73	2:26,44
6.	kusch, walter	ger	33,65	1:11,41	1:49,41	2:26,55
7.	cherdakov, igor	urs	33,28	1:10,38	1:48,49	2:27,15
8.	katzur, klaus	gdr	32,91	1:10,68	1:49,21	2:27,44

wr 2:22,8

WORLD CHAMPIONSHIPS

eptember 4th, 1973   **Belgrade**

00 metres breaststroke

ummary of heats

1	Hencken, John	USA	1:04.35w
2	Taguchi, Nobutaka	JAP	1:05.80
3	Pankin, Nikolay	URS	1:06.10
4	Colella, Rick	USA	1:06.72
5	Kriukin, Mikhail	URS	1:06.78
6	Wilkie, David	GBR	1:06.98
7	Glas, Jurgen	GDR	1:07.32
8	Cluer, Nigel	PNG	1:07.59
9	Michael, Gunther	GER	1:07.77
0	Combet, Bernard	FRA	1:08.26
1	Munoz, Felipe	MEX	1:08.37
2	Hrdlitschka, Peter	CAN	1:08.62
3	Balcells, Pedro	ESP	1:08.88
4	Wisloff, Ove	NOR	1:09.49
5	Dyrek, Pavel	POL	1:09.60
6	Szabo, Sandor	HUN	1:09.63
7	Hunger, Alfredo	PER	1:09.73
8	Pinto-Ribeiro, Sergio	BRA	1:09.80
9	Creswick, Michael	AUS	1:09.81
0	Nitzsche, Ullrich	GDR	1:09.87
1	Salcedo, Gustavo	MEX	1:09.92
2	Zajac, Mel	CAN	1:09.97
3	Divjak, Zdravko	YUG	1:10.15
4	Smiglak, Cezary	POL	1:10.57
5	Lalle, Giorgio	ITA	1:10.97
6	Kriechbaum, Steffen	AUT	1:11.06
7	Charkarov, A	BUL	1:11.29
8	Kerola, Tuomo	FIN	1:12.37
9	Nazario, C	PUR	1:13.33
0	Morkal, F	TUR	1:14.03
1	Catanchi, O	PUR	1:14.50
2	Ashhin, H	IRN	1:16.20

Result of final

1	Hencken, John	USA	1:04.02w/ch
2	Kriukin, Mikhail	URS	1:04.61e
3	Taguchi, Nobutaka	JAP	1:05.61
4	Wilkie, David	GBR	1:05.74c
5	Pankin, Nikolay	URS	1:06.55
6	Colella, Rick	USA	1:06.69
7	Glas, Jurgen	GDR	1:07.41
8	Cluer, Nigel	PNG	1:08.12

w = World record   ch = Championships record

e = European record   c = Commonwealth record

200 metres breaststroke

Summary of heats			100 m	200 m
1	Wilkie, David	GBR	1:08.84	2:20.94e/c
2	Hencken, John	USA	1:08.10	2:21.50
3	Cherdakov, Igor	URS	1:08.63	2:24.30
4	Kriukin, Mikhail	URS	1:09.23	2:24.85
5	Taguchi, Nobutaka	JAP	1:10.23	2:25.45
6	Cluer, Nigel	PNG	1:10.57	2:25.87
7	Colella, Rick	USA	1:11.27	2:26.17
8	Glas, Jurgen	GDR	1:11.73	2:27.77
9	Munoz, Felipe	MEX	1:11.62	2:28.34
10	Lalle, Giorgio	ITA	1:12.27	2:29.08
11	Wisloff, Ove	NOR	1:11.93	2:29.46
12	Balcells, Pedro	ESP	1:12.31	2:30.52
13	Nitzsche, Ullrich	GDR	1:11.86	2:31.01
14	Hrdlitschka, Peter	CAN	1:10.83	2:31.34
15	Kriechbaum, Steffen	AUT	1:14.11	2:31.56
16	Smiglak, Cezary	POL	1:12.23	2:32.50
17	Dyrek, Pavel	POL	1:13.49	2:32.66
18	Zajac, Mel	CAN	1:11.70	2:33.15
19	Creswick, Michael	AUS	1:10.81	2:33.61
20	Salcedo, Gustavo	MEX	1:11.65	2:33.99
21	Hunger, Alfredo	PER	1:14.33	2:34.78
22	Kerola, Tuomo	FIN	1:14.41	2:35.29
23	Combet, Bernard	FRA	1:13.13	2:35.34
24	Divjak, Zdravko	YUG	1:15.60	2:38.50
25	Catanchi, O	PUR	1:15:49	2:40.14
26	Nazario, C	PUR	1:17.61	2:43.79
27	Morkal, F	TUR	1:18.72	2:44.12
28	Ashhin, H	IRN	1:18.55	2:48.80

Result of final

1	Wilkie, David	GBR	1:07.56	2:19.28w/e/c/ch
2	Hencken, John	USA	1:06.78	2:19.95
3	Taguchi, Nobutaka	JAP	1:10.11	2:23.11
4	Kriukin, Mikhail	URS	1:07.07	2:23.47
5	Cluer, Nigel	PNG	1:09.37	2:25.87
6	Colella, Rick	USA	1:10.51	2:26.41
7	Glas, Jurgen	GDR	1:10.17	2:26.56
8	Cherdakov, Igor	URS	1:09.41	2:28.18

w = World record

ch = Championships record

e = European record

c = Commonwealth record

September 7th, 1973   **Belgrade**

200 metres medley

Summary of heats			100 m	200 m
1	Hargitay, Andras	HUN	1:01.38	2:09.54
2	Wilkie, David	GBR	1:02.19	2:09.61
3	Lietzmann, Christian	GDR	1:00.52	2:09.91
4	Larsson, Gunnar	SWE	1:01.12	2:10.13
5	Carper, Stan	USA	1:00.54	2:11.04
6	Zakharov, Sergey	URS	1:01.62	2:11.07
7	Tyler, Fred	USA	1:01.20	2:11.31
8	Sperling, Wolfram	GDR	1:03.60	2:11.46
9	Smirnov, Andrey	URS	1:02.36	2:11.98
10	Verraszto, Zoltan	HUN	1:00.51	2:12.65
11	Brinkley, Brian	GBR	1:04.25	2:14.31
12	Brumwell, Dave	CAN	1:03.05	2:14.99
13	Cluer, Nigel	PNG	1:05.85	2:15.90
14	Yanagikade, Tsuyoshi	JAP	1:03.33	2:16.01
15	Shirley. Brad	CAN	1:02.80	2:16.42
16	Delgado, Jorge	ECU	1:04.61	2:16.47
17	Orejuela, Eduardo	ECU	1:04.28	2:16.58
18	Martin, Neil	AUS	1:04.23	2:17.01
19	Marmolejo, Ricardo	MEX	1:04.54	2:17.05
20	Azevedo, Carlos	BRA	1:04.16	2:17.25
21	Gundersen, Gunnar	NOR	1:06.54	2:19.07
22	Tetlow, Peter	AUS	1:04.66	2:19.71
23	Volcan, Ramon	VEN	1:04.95	2:20.84
24	Santiago, Carlos	PUR	1:04.28	2:21.11
25	Jaramillo, Jorge	COL	1:05.32	2:21.39
26	Podolan, Harmut	AUT	1:04.89	2:21.72
27	Gharbi, A	TUN	1:05.05	2:22.62
28	Manochehr, C	IRN	1:16.40	2:38.93

Result of final

1	Larsson, Gunnar	SWE	1:00.32	2:08.36ch
2	Carper, Stan	USA	59.69	2:08.43
3	Wilkie, David	GBR	1:02.07	2:08.84c
4	Hargitay, Andras	HUN	1:00.24	2:09.52
5	Lietzmann, Christian	GDR	1:00.38	2:09.57
6	Sperling, Wolfram	GDR	1:03.49	2:10.54
7	Tyler, Fred	USA	1:01.76	2:10.86
8	Zakharov, Sergey	URS	1:01.45	2:10.86

ch = Championships record   c = Commonwealth record

September 9th, 1973   **Belgrade**

4 × 100 metres medley relay   **final**

After backstroke leg   **Split time**

1	GDR	Matthes, Roland	56.75
2	USA	Stamm, Mike	58.74
3	AUS	Cooper, Brad	59.66
4	GER	Steinbach, Klaus	59.69
5	CAN	MacKenzie, Ian	59.90
6	HUN	Cseh, Laszlo	1:00.31
7	GBR	Cunningham, Colin	1:00.60
8	URS	Grivennikov, Igor	1.01.09

After breaststroke leg

1	USA	Hencken, John	1:03.55	2:02.29
2	GDR	Glas, Jurgen	1:08.10	2:04.85
3	GBR	Wilkie, David	1:05.71	2:06.31
4	GER	Kusch, Walter	1:07.09	2:06.78
5	URS	Kriukin, Mikhail	1:05.78	2:06.87
6	HUN	Szabo, Sandor	1:07.56	2:07.87
7	CAN	Hrdlitschka, Peter	1:08.10	2:08.00
8	AUS	Creswick, Michael	1:09.12	2:08.78

After butterfly leg

1	USA	Bottom, Joe	55.93	2:58.22
2	GDR	Floeckner, Harmut	56.05	3:00.90
3	CAN	Robertson, Bruce	55.74	3:03.74
4	GER	Meeuw, Folkert	57.22	3:04.00
5	URS	Zakharov, Sergey	58.52	3:05.39
6	GBR	Edwards, Martin	59.58	3:05.89
7	HUN	Verraszto, Zoltan	58.65	3:06.52
8	AUS	Seymour, Ross	57.90	3:06.68

After freestyle leg

1	USA	Montgomery, Jim	51.27	3:49.49ch
2	GDR	Pyttel, Roger	52.34	3:53.24
3	CAN	Phillips, Brian	52.63	3:56.37
4	GER	Nocke, Peter	52.38	3:56.38
5	URS	Bure, Vladimir	52.70	3:58.09
6	AUS	Wenden, Mike	51.91	3:58.59
7	GBR	Brinkley, Brian	53.15	3:59.04
8	HUN	Szentirmay, Istvan	55.12	4:01.64

ch = Championships record

COMMONWEALTH GAMES

100 Metres Breaststroke **Christchurch**

Summary of heats (January 31, 1974)

1	Wilkie, David	SCO	1:07.78ch
2	Leigh, David	ENG	1:07.99
3	Naisby, Paul	ENG	1:08.15
4	Mahony, Bill	CAN	1:09.59
5	Cluer, Nigel	AUS	1:09.82
6	Hrdlitschka, Peter	CAN	1:10.10
7	Thomson, Alan	SCO	1:10.82
8	Bush, Gregory	AUS	1:11.29
9	Creswick, Michael	AUS	1:11.46
10	MacDonald, Gary	CAN	1:12.38
11	Lewis, Brent	NZL	1:12.70
12	Davies, Vivian	WAL	1:13.07
13	McGrory, Martin	NIR	1:13.10
14	Emslie, Julian	HKG	1:13.19
15	Corry, Ian	NIR	1:13.81
16	Tuoti, Usa	FIJ	1:29.37

Result of final (February 1, 1974)

1	Leigh, David	ENG	1:06.52ch
2	Wilkie, David	SCO	1:07.37
3	Naisby, Paul	ENG	1:08.52
4	Hrdlitschka, Peter	CAN	1:09.92
5	Cluer, Nigel	AUS	1:10.07
6	Thomson, Alan	SCO	1:10.69
7	Bush, Gregory	AUS	1:11.91
8	Creswick, Michael	AUS	1:15.43

Mahony of Canada did not swim in final

ch = Championships record

200 metres Breaststroke **Christchurch**

Summary of heats (January 26, 1974)			**100 m**	**200 m**
1	Leigh, David	ENG	1 : 10.26	2 : 26.29ch
2	Naisby, Paul	ENG	1 : 10.41	2 : 27.54
3	Mahony, Bill	CAN	1 : 12.66	2 : 28.09
4	Cluer, Nigel	AUS	1 : 12.15	2 : 28.72
5	Bush, Gregory	AUS	1 : 12.19	2 : 30.52
6	Wilkie, David	SCO	1 : 11.38	2 : 30.79
7	Hrdlitschka, Peter	CAN	1 : 11.94	2 : 32.42
8	Creswick, Michael	AUS	1 : 13.06	2 : 33.89
9	Thomson, Alan	SCO	1 : 12.46	2 : 33.92
10	Lewis, Brent	NZL	1 : 13.44	2 : 34.94
11	Davies, Vivian	WAL	1 : 13.59	2 : 35.67
12	Corry, Ian	NZL	1 : 14.71	2 : 36.49
13	MacDonald, Gary	CAN	1 : 14.65	2 : 38.19
14	McGrory, Martin	NIR	1 : 13.58	2 : 39.26
15	Emslie, Julian	HKG	1 : 18.58	2 : 41.84
16	Tuoti, Usa	FIJ	1 : 22.97	2 : 57.29

Result of final (January 30, 1974)

1	Wilkie, David	SCO	1:09.86	2:24.42ch
2	Leigh, David	ENG	1:10.11	2:24.75
3	Naisby, Paul	ENG	1:10.52	2:27.36
4	Mahony, Bill	CAN	1:11.77	2:27.62
5	Bush, Gregory	AUS	1:11.55	2:30.13
6	Cluer, Nigel	AUS	1:11.73	2:30.56
7	Hrdlitschka, Peter	CAN	1:12.95	2:32.92
8	Creswick, Michael	AUS	1:12.42	2:37.31

ch = Championships record

200 metres Medley   **Christchurch**

Summary of heats (January 28, 1974)   **100 m**   **200 m**

1	MacDonald, Gary	CAN	1:02.38	2:12.91ch
2	Wilkie, David	SCO	1:04.52	2:14.39
3	Terrell, Ray	ENG	1:02.75	2:14.54
4	Cluer, Nigel	AUS	1:05.11	2:15.89
5	Brinkley, Brian	ENG	1:04.03	2:16.09
6	Naisby, Paul	ENG	1:05.87	2:16.54
7	Jones, Rowland	WAL	1:04.75	2:17.83
8	Hrdlitschka, Peter	CAN	1:05.63	2:18.55
9	Carter, Jimmy	SCO	1:05.44	2:19.35
10	Kulasalu, John	AUS	1:05.67	2:19.46
11	Fogel, Ashley	NZL	1:04.87	2:19.84
12	Davies, Vivian	WAL	1:07.04	2:21.63
13	Kemmet, Lorne	CAN	1:05.48	2:23.22
14	Choon Chiang, Jin	MSA	1:06.11	2:26.00

Result of final (January 30, 1974)

1	Wilkie, David	SCO	1:01.89	2:10.11ch
2	Brinkley, Brian	ENG	1:02.74	2:12.73
3	MacDonald, Gary	CAN	1:02.46	2:12.98
4	Terrell, Ray	ENG	1:01.86	2:13.69
5	Cluer, Nigel	AUS	1:05.45	2:15.00
6	Jones, Rowland	WAL		2:17.83
7	Hrdlitschka, Peter	CAN	1:05.41	2:17.84
8	Carter, Jimmy	SCO		2:18.74

Naisby of England did not swim in final

ch = Championships record

EUROPEAN CHAMPIONSHIPS

August 23, 1974   **Vienna**

200 metres breaststroke

Summary of heats			**100 m**	**200 m**
1	Pankin, Nikolay	URS	1:09.94	2:24.00
2	Wilkie, David	GBR	1:09.13	2:24.37
3	Leigh, David	GBR	1:08.68	2:25.10
4	Lalle, Giorgio	ITA	1:11.28	2:25.57
5	Kriukin, Mikhail	URS	1:08.26	2:26.01
6	Kusch, Walter	GER	1:11.97	2:27.36
7	Wisloff, Ove	NOR	1:08.90	2:27.41
8	Kriechbaum, Steffen	AUT	1:10.24	2:27.70
9	Glas, Jurgen	GDR	1:12.04	2:28.98
10	Paehr, Thomas	GER	1:10.89	2:29.16
11	Walter, Jorge	GDR	1:12.88	2:29.37
12	Andersson, Stefan	SWE	1:11.95	2:29.64
13	Mauro, Ginacarlo	ITA	1:11.14	2:30.43
14	Christensen, Glen	SWE	1:13.03	2:31.01
15	Dubey, Jean-Pierre	SUI	1:11.74	2:31.60
16	Kerola, Tuomo	FIN	1:12.12	2:31.64
17	Vingherhoets, Rudi	BEL	1:13.83	2:33.21
18	Splawinsky, Andrey	POL	1:12.00	2:33.60
19	Combet, Bernard	FRA	1:12.23	2:34.12
20	Gay, Jacques	FRA	1:13.90	2:36.01
21	Divjak, Zdravko	YUG	1:15.33	2:40.57
22	Oliveira, Carlos	POR	1:19.96	2:46.68

Result of final				
1	Wilkie, David	GBR	1:11.29	2:20.42 ch
2	Pankin, Nikolay	URS	1:11.23	2:22.84 n
3	Leigh, David	GBR	1:11.69	2:23.79
4	Kriukin, Mikhail	URS	1:11.28	2:24.73
5	Kusch, Walter	GFR	1:10.84	2:25.29
6	Lalle, Giorgio	ITA	1:12.01	2:25.94
7	Kriechbaum, Steffen	AUT	1:10.16	2:27.37
disq	Wisloff, Ove	NOR		

ch = Championships record

n = National record

August 24, 1974   **Vienna**

200 metres medley

Summary of Heats

1	Wilkie, David	GBR	2:08.48 ch/n
2	Lietzmann, Christian	GDR	2:08.71
3	Smirnov, Andrey	URS	2:09.29 n
4	Hargitay, Andras	HUN	2:09.64
5	Zaharov, Sergey	URS	2:10.80
6	Verraszto, Zoltan	HUN	2:10.99
7	Sperling, Wolfram	GDR	2:11.53
8	Esteva, Santiago	ESP	2:12.43 n
9	Koenneker, Jurgen	GER	2:13.13
10	Melberg, Atle	NOR	2:13.43
11	Marugo, Lorenzo	ITA	2:14.60
12	Barelli, Paolo	ITA	2:15.68
13	Gundersen, Gunnar	NOR	2:15.99
14	Deley, Francois	BEL	2:17.38
15	Gjukez, Franz	AUT	2:19.26
16	Rasmussen, Henrik	DEN	2:20.62
17	Stoev, Ludmil	BUL	2:21.76
18	Kerola, Tuomo	FIN	2:22.55
19	Coyle, Desmond	IRL	2.23.62
20	Wilwert, Josy	LUX	2:24.63

Result of final

1	Wilkie, David	GBR	2:06.32 w/e/c
2	Lietzmann, Christian	GDR	2:07.61 n
3	Hargitay, Andras	HUN	2:09.08 n
4	Smirnov, Andrey	URS	2:09.17 n
5	Zaharov, Sergey	URS	2:09.96
6	Verraszto, Zoltan	HUN	2:11.23
7	Sperling, Wolfram	GDR	2:11.56
8	Esteva, Santiago	ESP	2:12.45

w = World record

e = European record

n = National record

c = Commonwealth record

ch = Championships record

Wilkie

4 × 100 metres medley relay   **final**

After backstroke leg   **Split Time**

1	GDR	Matthes, Roland	57.79
2	GER	Steinbach, Klaus	58.56 n
3	ESP	Esteva, Santiago	59.73
4	HUN	Verraszto, Zoltan	59.77
5	GBR	Cunningham, Colin	59.82 n
6	URS	Potjakin, Igor	1:00.53
7	ITA	Cianchi, Lapo	1:01.50
8	FRA	Meslier, Franck	1:02.93

After breaststroke leg

1	GER	Kusch, Walter	1:04.63	2:03.19
2	GBR	Wilkie, David	1:03.61	2:03.43
3	URS	Pankin, Nikolay	1:04.75	2:05.28
4	GDR	Lietzmann, Christian	1:07.80	2:05.59
5	ESP	Balcells, Pedro	1:08.19	2:07.92
6	ITA	Lalle, Giorgio	1:06.60	2:08.10
7	HUN	Szabo, Sandor	1:08.50	2:08.27
8	FRA	Combet, Bernard	1:07.16	2:10.09

After butterfly leg

1	GER	Meeuw, Folkert	56.65	2:59.84
2	GDR	Pyttel, Roger	55.41	3:01.00
3	GBR	Nash, Steve	58.18	3:01.61
4	URS	Sharygin, Viktor	56.89	3:02.17
5	ESP	Lang-Lenton, Arturo	57.73	3:05.65
6	HUN	Hargitay, Andras	57.69	3:05.96
7	ITA	Barelli, Paolo	58.23	3:06.33
8	FRA	Buttet, Serge	58.84	3:08.93

After freestyle leg

1	GER	Nocke, Peter	51.73	3:51.57 e
2	GBR	Brinkley, Brian	52.52	3:54.13 n
3	URS	Bure, Vladimir	52.20	3:54.37
4	GDR	Hartung, Wilfried	53.63	3:54.63
5	ITA	Pangaro, Roberto	52.17	3:58.50
6	ESP	Comas, Jorge	53.50	3:59.15
7	HUN	Hamori, Jeno	54.51	4:00.47
8	FRA	Rousseau, Michel	52.41	4:01.34

e = European record   n = National record

WORLD CHAMPIONSHIPS

July 22nd. 1975   **Cali**

MEN   100m BREASTSTROKE/PECHO   HOMBRES

HEAT 1		50m	100m
1 Wilkie, David	GBR	31.64	1:06.40
2 Smith, Graham	CAN	31.71	1:07.33
3 Kabatani, Hiroshi	JPN	32.52	1:08.82
4 Chevalier, Camil	CAN	31.92	1:08.88
5 Norling, Anders	SWE	32.34	1:09.12
6 Kriechbaum, Steffen	AUT	32.80	1:10.64
7 Calderon, Victor	ECU	35.93	1:17.31

HEAT 2			
1 Pankin, Nicolai	URS	31.61	1:06.32
2 Leigh, David	GBR	31.49	1.06.46
3 Combet, Bernard	FRA	31.31	1:06.77
4 Ribeiro, Sergio	BRA	31.67	1:07.52
5 Divjak, Zdravko	YUG	31.54	1:08.43
6 Glas, Jurgen	GDR	32.62	1:09.80
7 Orozco, Jacinto	ECU	34.41	1:15.34

HEAT 3			
1 Kusch, Walter	GFR	31.76	1:06.32
2 Lang, Peter	GFR	31.52	1:06.85
3 Lalle, Giorgio	ITA	31.91	1:07.07
4 Khrukin, Mikhail	URS	31.73	1:07.09
5 Arnicke, Gregor	GDR	32.34	1:07.74
6 Kerola, Tuomo	FIN	32.67	1:09.21
7 Restrepo, Pablo	COL	34.79	1.13.41

HEAT 4			
1 Hofstetter, Rick	USA	30.87	1:06.07
2 Colella, Rick	USA	31.49	1:06.13
3 Taguchi, Nobutaka	JPN	31.35	1:06.40
4 Wisloff, Ove	NOR	32.17	1:07.71
5 Christiansen, Glen	SWE	31.57	1:08.08
6 Ferracuti, Peiro	SAL	32.77	1:10.14
7 Sierra, Fernando	COL	33.22	1.12.07

FINAL			
1 Wilkie, David	GBR	30.73	1:04.26
2 Taguchi, Nobutaka	JPN	30.57	1:05 04
3 Leigh, David	GBR	30.42	1:05.32
4 Colella, Rick	USA	31.26	1:05.56
5 Pankin, Nicolai	URS	31.01	1:05.71
6 Kusch, Walter	GFR	32.05	1:05.76
7 Hofstetter, Rick	USA	30.90	1:05.96
8 Combet, Bernard	FRA	31.49	1:06.80

July 24th, 1975 **Cali**

MEN 200m BREASTSTROKE/PECHO HOMBRES

HEAT 1		50m	100m	150m	200m
1 Wilkie, David	GBR	32.53	1:09.16	1:45.05	2:21.90
2 Leigh, David	GBR	32.26	1:08.96	1:46.52	2:25.04
3 Heinbuch, David	CAN	33.95	1:11.67	1:50.57	2:30.78
4 Ferracuti, Piero	SAL	33.95	1:11.78	1:51.31	2:32.19
5 Divjak, Zdravko	YUG	34.71	1:14.00	1:53.16	2:32.80
6 Calderon, Victor	ECU	37.53	1:22.07	2:07.49	2:52.31

HEAT 2					
1 Taguchi, Nobutaka	JPN	33.55	1:11.18	1:48.50	2:25.25
2 Smith, Graham	CAN	33.78	1:11.64	1:48.94	2:25.42
3 Norling, Anders	SWE	34.40	1:11.93	1:49.33	2:26.72
4 Krhukin, Mikhail	URS	33.46	1:11.16	1:48.87	2:27.46
5 Arnicke, Gregor	GDR	34.20	1:13.04	1:50.93	2:29.49
6 Kabatani, Hiroshi	JPN	34.51	1:13.38	1:52.97	2:31.85
7 Orozco, Jacinto	ECU	36.30	1:18.91	2:04.36	2:49.30

HEAT 3					
1 Pankin, Nicolai	URS	33.48	1:09.95	1:46.59	2:24.29
2 Bohan, Rick	USA	32.27	1:08.38	1:46.72	2:27.10
3 Ribeiro, Sergio	BRA	32.82	1:10.54	1:48.88	2:28.03
3 Wisloff, Ove	NOR	32.88	1:09.74	1:48.30	2:28.03
5 Balcells, Pedro	ESP	33.68	1:11.22	1:49.64	2:28.91
6 Christiansen, Glen	SWE	34.16	1:11.67	1:50.60	2:30.00
7 Villalobos, Fernd.	COL	36.16	1:17.58	1:59.48	2:42.51

HEAT 4					
1 Colella, Rick	USA	32.99	1:09.30	1:45.59	2:22.83
2 Kusch, Walter	GFR	34.26	1:11.11	1:47.76	2:23.90
3 Lalle, Giorgio	ITA	33.42	1:10.88	1:48.08	2:26.16
4 Glas, Jurgen	GDR	33.70	1:11.69	1:50.88	2:30.20
5 Hamacher, Jorg	GFR	34.17	1:12.56	1:51.90	2:31.12
6 Kerola, Tuomo	FIN	34.01	1:11.96	1:51.35	2:31.52
7 Sierra, Fernando	COL	35.30	1:15.81	1:56.94	2:38.17

FINAL					
1 Wilkie, David	GBR	31.74	1:07.60	1:42.46	*2:18.23
2 Colella, Rick	USA	32.39	1:08.48	1:44.30	2:21.60
3 Pankin, Nicolai	URS	33.30	1:09.54	1:45.39	2:21.75
4 Kusch, Walter	GFR	32.83	1:10.05	1:45.98	2:22.68
5 Leigh David	GBR	32.43	1:09.69	1:46.46	2:23.38
6 Taguchi, Nobutaka	JPN	32.60	1:09.51	1:46.21	2:24.08
7 Smith, Graham	CAN	33.03	1:10.48	1:46.99	2:24.13
8 Lalle, Giorgio	ITA	33.11	1:09.88	1:47.20	2:24.98

MEN   200m MEDLEY/COMBINADO   HOMBRES

HEAT 1		50m	100m	150m	200m
1 Smirnov, Andrei	URS	28.41	1:02.25	1:39.67	2:09.87
2 Zakharov, Sergei	URS	29.16	1:02.51	1:40.84	2:11.40
3 Buren, John van	CAN	28.09	1:00.83	1:42.32	2:12.92
4 Marugo, Lorenzo	ITA	29.52	1:03.77	1:42.68	2:13.96
5 Jameson, Gary	GBR	29.32	1:02.95	1:43.03	2:14.72
6 Dawson, Peter	AUS	29.55	1:03.94	1:43.58	2:15.38

HEAT 2					
1 Verraszto, Zoltan	HUN	28.52	1:00.87	1:41.38	2:11.04
2 Tyler, Fred	USA	28.09	1:01.86	1:41.16	2:11.16
3 Windeatt, Graham	AUS	28.52	1:02.77	1:42.05	2:12.34
4 Becker, Reinhold	GFR	29.44	1:03.89	1:44.54	2:16.42
5 Pickell, Steve	CAN	28.09	1:01.78	1:44.34	2:16.78
6 Sierra, German	COL	29.18	1:06.28	1:50.94	2:23.90
7 Ledesma, Enrique	ECU	30.36	1:07.38	1:50.29	2:25.13

HEAT 3					
1 Hargitay, Andras	HUN	28.04	1:00.70	1:39.39	2:09.16
2 Furniss, Steve	USA	27.40	1:00.15	1:39.62	2:09.48
3 Esteva, Santiago	ESP	28.40	1:00.97	1:41.85	2:11.94
4 Wilkie, David	GBR	28.56	1:02.98	1:40.18	2:12.68
5 Sasaki, Jiro	JPN	28.95	1:03.29	1:43.52	2:14.28
6 Bohmert, Steffen	GDR	29.03	1:04.07	1:43.57	2:14.93
7 Hsu Tun Hsiung	ROC	29.20	1:04.05	1:47.03	2:20.25

FINAL					
1 Hargitay, Andras	HUN	27.54	59.86	1:38.20	*2:07.72
2 Furniss, Steve	USA	27.37	59.54	1:38.56	2:07.75
3 Smirnov, Andrei	URS	27.79	1:01.58	1:38.67	2:08.52
4 Tyler, Fred	USA	27.70	1:01.10	1:39.43	2:09.12
5 Verraszto, Zoltan	HUN	27.95	59.61	1:39.24	2:09.44
6 Zakharov, Sergei	URS	28.59	1:01.70	1:40.23	2:10.75
7 Windeatt, Graham	AUS	28.59	1:02.76	1:42.42	2:12.66
8 Esteva, Santiago	ESP	27.96	1:01.20	1:43.48	2:15.14

July 27th, 1975 **Cali**

4 × 100 metres medley relay **men** **final**

After backstroke leg Split time

1	USA	Murphy, John	57.81
2	CAN	Pickell, Steve	58.23
3	GDR	Matthes, Roland	58.43
4	GER	Steinbach, Klaus	58.95
5	ESP	Esteva, Santiago	59.57
6	ITA	Cianchi, Lapo	1:00.44
7	GBR	Carter, Jimmy	1:00.78
8	URS	Omeltshenko, Igor	1:01.69

After breaststroke leg

1	USA	Colella, Rick	1:04.71	2:02.52
2	GER	Kusch, Walter	1:04.50	2:03.45
3	GBR	Wilkie, David	1:03.49	2:04.27
4	CAN	Smith, Graham	1:06.80	2:05.03
5	GDR	Arnicke, Gregor	1:07.74	2:06.17
6	ITA	Lalle, Giorgio	1:05.01	2:06.67
7	URS	Pankin, Nikolay	1:06.23	2:06.70
8	ESP	Balcells, Pedro	1:07.58	2:07.15

After butterfly leg

1	USA	Jagenburg, Greg	55.75	2:58.27
2	GBR	Brinkley, Brian	55.55	2:59.82
3	GER	Kraus, Michael	56.71	3:00.16
4	CAN	Robertson, Bruce	56.57	3:01.60
5	GDR	Pyttel, Roger	55.98	3:02.15
6	URS	Manatshinski, Alexandr	56.95	3:03.65
7	ITA	Barelli, Paolo	58.14	3:04.81
8	ESP	Bonnet, Jose	58.40	3:05.55

After freestyle leg

1	USA	Coan, Andy	50.73	3:49.00ch
2	GER	Nocke, Peter	51.69	3:51.85
3	GBR	Downie, Gordon	52.98	3:52.80
4	CAN	Kasting, Bob	52.28	3:53.88
5	GDR	Wanja, Lutz	53.29	3:55.44
6	URS	Bure, Vladimir	51.93	3:55.58
7	ITA	Guarducci, Marcello	52.01	3:56.82
8	ESP	Comas, Jorge	53.84	3:59.39

ch = Championships record

OLYMPIC GAMES—MONTREAL

```
piscine olympique          july 19 juil   11:00    resultats / results
natation             100 m brasse         hommes          eliminatoire 1
swimming             100 m breaststroke    men            heat 1
ro/or=  1:04.94      rm/wr= 1:03.88      date/hr: 19/11:05   appr:  glk
```

rang rank	coul lane				50 m	100 m	
1	4	128	goodhew,duncan	gbr	30.69	1:04.92	nro nor
2	5	394	pankin,nikolay	urs	30.79	1:05.38	
3	3	310	wisloeff,ove	nor	31.31	1:06.85	
4	6	272	shinya,tateki	jpn	31.62	1:07.59	
5	7	320	smiglak,cezary	pol	31.64	1:08.02	
6	2	80	zajac,mel	can	31.46	1:08.52	
7	1	302	knoepffler,campari	nca	35.41	1:15.18	

```
piscine olympique          july 19 juil   11:00    resultats / results
natation             100 m brasse         hommes          eliminatoire 2
swimming             100 m breaststroke    men            heat 2
ro/or=  1:04.94      rm/wr= 1:03.88      date/hr: 19/11:11   appr:  glk
```

rang rank	coul lane				50 m	100 m	
1	5	377	iuozaytis,arvidas	urs	30.42	1:04.78	nro nor
2	3	169	lang,peter	ger	31.07	1:05.25	
3	4	167	kusch,walter	ger	31.59	1:05.88	
4	2	28	kriechbaum,steffen	aut	32.11	1:08.09	
5	7	107	kerola,tuomo	fin	32.50	1:08.22	
6	6	333	nazario,carlos	pur	31.96	1:08.33	
7	1	323	carvalhovicencio,henrique	por	34.53	1:13.55	

```
piscine olympique          july 19 juil   11:00    resultats / results
natation             100 m brasse         hommes          eliminatoire 3
swimming             100 m breaststroke    men            heat 3
ro/or=  1:04.94      rm/wr= 1:03.88      date/hr: 19/11:17   appr:  glk
```

rang rank	coul lane				50 m	100 m
1	6	131	leigh,david	gbr	31.21	1:06.12
2	5	259	lalle,giorgio	ita	31.86	1:06.38
3	7	359	norling,anders	swe	31.52	1:06.52
4	4	372	dementiev,vladimir	urs	31.43	1:06.96
5	2	290	lozano,gustavo	mex	32.16	1:08.89
6	1	213	javor,istvan	hun		np
6	3	151	sperling,wolfram	gdr		np

```
piscine olympique          july 19 juil   11:00    resultats / resuits
natation             100 m brasse         hommes          eliminatoire 4
swimming             100 m breaststroke    men            heat 4
ro/or=  1:04.94      rm/wr= 1:03.88      date/hr: 19/11:23   appr:  glk
```

rang rank	coul lane				50 m	100 m
1	4	143	wilkie,david	gbr	31.16	1:05.19
1	5	78	smith,graham	can	30.71	1:05.19
3	3	412	dowler,lawrence	usa	30.72	1:05.32
4	6	40	p. ribeiro,sergio	bra	31.36	1:06.07
5	2	97	balcells,pedro	esp	31.94	1:07.98
6	7	32	knowles,bruce	bah	33.73	1:11.65
7	1	338	wang,c chun	roc		np

```
piscine olympique              july 19 juil   11:00    resultats / results
natation               100 m brasse           hommes           eliminatoire 5
swimming               100 m breaststroke     men              heat 5
ro/or= 1:04.94         rm/wr= 1:03.88         date/hr: 19/11:36  corr:  dnb
```

rang rank	coul lane				50 m	100 m	
1	4	422	hencken,john	usa	29.89	1:03.88	erm ewr
2	5	273	taguchi,nobutaka	jpn	30.31	1:04.65	
3	3	436	woo,chris	usa	30.34	1:05.39	
4	6	36	fiolo,jose s	bra	31.01	1:06.18	
5	2	8	jarvie,paul	aus	31.18	1:06.22	
6	7	447	divjak,zdravko	yug	31.62	1:08.31	
7	1	440	sochasky,glen	ven	32.85	1:09.93	
8	8	116	pierre,bernard	fra		np	

```
piscine olympique              july 19 juil   11:00    resultats / results
natation               100 m brasse           hommes           sommaire/eliminatoires
swimming               100 m breaststroke     men              summary/heats
ro/or= 1:04.94         rm/wr= 1:03.88         date/hr: 26/17:25  appr:  aut
```

rang rank	coul lane				50 m	100 m	
1	4	422	hencken,john	usa	29.89	1:03.88	erm ewr
2	5	273	taguchi,nobutaka	jpn	30.31	1:04.65	
3	5	377	iuozaytis,arvidas	urs	30.42	1:04.78	
4	4	128	goodhew,duncan	gbr	30.69	1:04.92	
5	4	143	wilkie,david	gbr	31.16	1:05.19	
5	5	78	smith,graham	can	30.71	1:05.19	
7	3	169	lang,peter	ger	31.07	1:05.25	
8	3	412	dowler,lawrence	usa	30.72	1:05.32	
9	5	394	pankin,nikolay	urs	30.79	1:05.38	
10	3	436	woo,chris	usa	30.34	1:05.39	
11	4	167	kusch,walter	ger	31.59	1:05.88	
12	6	40	p. ribeiro,sergio	bra	31.36	1:06.07	
13	6	131	leigh,david	gbr	31.21	1:06.12	
14	6	36	fiolo,jose s.	bra	31.01	1:06.18	
15	2	8	jarvie,paul	aus	31.18	1:06.22	
16	9	259	lalle,giorgio	ita	31.86	1:06.38	
17	7	359	norling,anders	swe	31.52	1:06.52	
18	3	310	wisloeff,ove	nor	31.31	1:06.85	
19	4	372	dementiev,vladimir	urs	31.43	1:06.96	
20	6	272	shinya,tateki	jpn	31.62	1:07.59	
21	2	97	balcells,pedro	esp	31.94	1:07.98	
22	7	320	smiglak,cezary	pol	31.64	1:08.02	
23	2	28	kriechbaum,steffen	aut	32.11	1:08.09	
24	7	107	kerola,tuomo	fin	32.50	1:08.22	
25	7	447	divjak,zdravko	yug	31.62	1:08.31	
26	6	333	nazario,carlos	pur	31.96	1:08.33	
27	2	80	zajac,mel	can	31.46	1:08.52	
28	2	290	lozano,gustavo	mex	32.16	1:08.89	
29	1	440	sochasky,glen	ven	32.85	1:09.93	
30	7	32	knowles,bruce	bah	33.73	1:11.65	
31	1	323	carvalhovicencio,henrique	por	34.53	1:13.55	
32	1	302	knoepffler,campari	nca	35.41	1:15.18	
33	1	213	javor,istvan	hun		np	
33	3	151	sperling,wolfram	gdr		np	
33	1	338	wang,c chun	roc		np	
33	8	116	pierre,bernard	fra		np	

les seize premiers se qualifient pour la demi-finale
the first sixteen qualify for the semi-final

```
piscine olympique          july 19 juil   19:00    resultats / results
natation              100 m brasse        hommes            demi-finale 1
swimming              100 m breaststroke  men               semi-final 1
ro/or=  1:03.88       rm/wr= 1:03.88      date/hr: 19/19:15  appr:  glk

rang  coul                                        50 m        100 m
rank  lane

 1     3      143  wilkie,david          gbr     30.70      1:04.29
 2     8      259  lalle,giorgio         ita     30.40      1:04.35
 3     5      128  goodhew,duncan        gbr     30.62      1:04.59
 4     2      436  woo,chris             usa     30.45      1:04.86
 5     6      412  dowler,lawrence       usa     30.83      1:05.19
 6     4      273  taguchi,nobutaka      jpn     30.91      1:05.69
 7     1       36  fiolo,jose s.         bra     30.54      1:06.38
 8     7       40  p. ribeiro,sergio     bra     31.76      1:06.69
```

```
piscine olympique          july 19 juil   19:00    resultats / results
natation              100 m brasse        hommes            demi-finale 2
swimming              100 m breaststroke  men               semi-final 2
ro/or=  1:03.88       rm/wr= 1:03.88      date/hr: 19/19:23  appr:  glk

rang  coul                                        50 m        100 m
rank  lane

 1     4      422  hencken,john          usa     30.00      1:03.62 nrm nwr
 2     3       78  smith,graham          can     30.51      1:03.92
 3     7      167  kusch,walter          ger     30.64      1:04.28
 4     5      377  iuozaytis,arvidas     urs     30.37      1:04.76
 5     6      169  lang,peter            ger     30.70      1:05.19
 6     2      394  pankin,nikolay        urs     30.63      1:05.59
 7     1      131  leigh,david           gbr     31.01      1:05.91
 8     8        8  jarvie,paul           aus     31.50      1:06.20
```

```
piscine olympique          july 19 juil   19:00    resultats / results
natation              100 m brasse        hommes        sommaire/demi-finales
swimming              100 m breaststroke  men           summary/semi-finals
ro/or=  1:03.88       rm/wr= 1:03.88      date/hr: 26/17:28  appr:  aut

rang  coul                                        50 m        100 m
rank  lane

 1     4      422  hencken,john          usa     30.00      1:03.62 nrm nwr
 2     3       78  smith,graham          can     30.51      1:03.92
 3     7      167  kusch,walter          ger     30.64      1:04.28
 4     3      143  wilkie,david          gbr     30.70      1:04.29
 5     8      259  lalle,giorgio         ita     30.40      1:04.35
 6     5      128  goodhew,duncan        gbr     30.62      1:04.59
 7     5      377  iuozaytis,arvidas     urs     30.37      1:04.76
 8     2      436  woo,chris             usa     30.45      1:04.86
 9     6      412  dowler,lawrence       usa     30.83      1:05.19
 9     6      169  lang,peter            ger     30.70      1:05.19
11     2      394  pankin,nikolay        urs     30.63      1:05.59
12     4      273  taguchi,nobutaka      jpn     30.91      1:05.69
13     1      131  leigh,david           gbr     31.01      1:05.91
14     8        8  jarvie,paul           aus     31.50      1:06.20
15     1       36  fiolo,jose s.         bra     30.54      1:06.38
16     7       40  p. ribeiro,sergio     bra     31.76      1:06.69
```

les huit premiers se qualifient pour la finale
the first eight qualify for the final

```
piscine olympique          july 20 juil   20:00   resultats / results
natation                  100 m brasse          hommes           finale
swimming                  100 m breaststroke    men              final
ro/or= 1:03.62            rm/wr= 1:03.62        date/hr: 20/20:44  fin:   glk
```

rang rank	coul lane					50 m	100 m
1	4	422	hencken,john		usa	29.48	1:03.11 nrm nwr
2	6	143	wilkie,david		gbr	30.45	1:03.43
3	1	377	iuozaytis,arvidas		urs	30.31	1:04.23
4	5	78	smith,graham		can	30.29	1:04.26
5	2	259	lalle,giorgio		ita	30.09	1:04.37
6	3	167	kusch,walter		ger	30.38	1:04.38
7	7	128	goodhew,duncan		gbr	30.47	1:04.66
8	8	436	woo,chris		usa	30.67	1:05.13

```
piscine olympique          july 24 juil   10:30   resultats / results
natation                  200 m brasse          hommes           eliminatoire 1
swimming                  200 m breaststroke    men              heat 1
ro/or= 2:21.55            rm/wr= 2:18.21        date/hr: 24/11:05  corr:  glk
```

rang rank	coul lane					50 m	100 m	150 m	200 m
1	4	78	smith,graham		can	32.85	1:09.42	1:45.91	2:22.24
2	5	377	iuozaytis,arvidas		urs	33.39	1:10.23	1:47.25	2:22.59
3	6	359	norling,anders		swe	33.39	1:10.39	1:46.77	2:24.61
4	7	169	lang,peter		ger	32.69	1:09.95	1:47.79	2:24.96
5	2	107	kerola,tuomo		fin	33.38	1:10.35	1:47.82	2:25.87
6	8	317	abreu,emilio j.		par	35.10	1:13.70	1:54.08	2:35.22
7	3	40	p. ribeiro,sergio		bra				dq
8	1	151	sperling,wolfram		gdr				np

```
piscine olympique          july 24 juil   10:30   resultats / results
natation                  200 m brasse          hommes           eliminatoire 2
swimming                  200 m breaststroke    men              heat 2
ro/or= 2:21.55            rm/wr= 2:18.21        date/hr: 24/10:59  appr:  glk
```

rang rank	coul lane					50 m	100 m	150 m	200 m
1	4	409	colella,rick		usa	33.28	1:09.75	1:45.32	2:21.08 nro nor
2	5	394	pankin,nikolay		urs	33.69	1:10.04	1:46.07	2:22.82
3	3	259	lalle,giorgio		ita	33.50	1:09.79	1:46.44	2:23.63
4	6	131	leigh,david		gbr	33.60	1:10.53	1:47.65	2:25.58
5	7	272	shinya,tateki		jpn	34.06	1:10.99	1:48.48	2:26.16
6	1	290	lozano,gustavo		mex	33.38	1:11.61	1:51.46	2:31.89
7	2	333	nazario,carlos		pur				dq

```
piscine olympique          july 24 juil   10:30   resultats / results
natation                  200 m brasse          hommes           eliminatoire 3
swimming                  200 m breaststroke    men              heat 3
ro/or= 2:21.55            rm/wr= 2:18.21        date/hr: 24/11:03  appr:  glk
```

rang rank	coul lane					50 m	100 m	150 m	200 m
1	4	422	hencken,john		usa	31.93	1:07.33	1:43.96	2:21.23
2	6	167	kusch,walter		ger	33.06	1:09.52	1:46.66	2:22.95
3	3	273	taguchi,nobutaka		jpn	32.65	1:09.81	1:46.86	2:24.12
4	2	59	heinbuch,dave		can	33.41	1:10.04	1:46.97	2:25.29
5	7	28	kriechbaum,steffen		aut	32.90	1:10.21	1:47.48	2:25.73
6	1	8	jarvie,paul		aus	33.89	1:11.37	1:50.35	2:30.15
7	8	323	carvalhovicencio,henrique		por	36.24	1:17.85	1:59.89	2:41.97
8	5	222	vermes,alban		hun				np

```
piscine olympique          july 24 juil   10:30   resultats / results
natation              200 m brasse         hommes          eliminatoire 4
swimming              200 m breaststroke    men            heat 4
ro/or=  2:21.55        rm/wr= 2:18.21    date/hr: 24/11:15   appr: glk

rang  coul                                  50 m    100 m    150 m     200 m
rank  lane

 1    4    143 wilkie,david          gbr   31.70   1:06.88  1:42.54  2:18.29 nro nor
 2    3    424 keating,charles       usa   32.52   1:08.36  1:44.59  2:22.22
 3    5    385 kudis,aygar           urs   32.58   1:09.31  1:46.86  2:23.45
 4    6    310 wisloeff,ove          nor   32.47   1:08.72  1:45.72  2:23.49
 5    1    332 gatinchi,orlando      pur   33.70   1:11.54  1:48.92  2:26.27
 6    7    320 smiglak,cezary        pol   33.14   1:10.12  1:47.96  2:27.41
 7    8    447 divjak,zdravko        yug   36.12   1:15.57  1:54.51  2:34.07
 8    2    136 naisby,paul           gbr                             dq
```

```
piscine olympique          july 24 juil   10:30   resultats / results
natation              200 m brasse         hommes       sommaire/eliminatoires
swimming              200 m breaststroke    men            summary/heats
ro/or=  2:21.55        rm/wr= 2:18.21    date/hr: 24/11:17   appr: jeq

rang  coul                                  50 m    100 m    150 m     200 m
rank  lane

 1    4    143 wilkie,david             gbr   31.70   1:06.88  1:42.54  2:18.29 nro nor
 2    4    409 colella,rick             usa   33.28   1:09.75  1:45.32  2:21.08
 3    4    422 hencken,john             usa   31.93   1:07.33  1:43.96  2:21.23
 4    3    424 keating,charles          usa   32.52   1:08.36  1:44.59  2:22.22
 5    4     78 smith,graham             can   32.85   1:09.42  1:45.91  2:22.24
 6    5    377 iuozaytis,arvidas        urs   33.39   1:10.23  1:47.25  2:22.59
 7    5    394 pankin,nikolay           urs   33.69   1:10.04  1:46.07  2:22.82
 8    6    167 kusch,walter             ger   33.06   1:09.52  1:46.66  2:22.95
 9    5    385 kudis,aygar              urs   32.58   1:09.31  1:46.86  2:23.45
10    6    310 wisloeff,ove             nor   32.47   1:08.72  1:45.72  2:23.49
11    3    259 lalle,giorgio            ita   33.50   1:09.79  1:46.44  2:23.63
12    3    273 taguchi,nobutaka         jpn   32.65   1:09.81  1:46.86  2:24.12
13    6    359 norling,anders           swe   33.39   1:10.39  1:46.77  2:24.61
14    7    169 lang,peter               ger   32.69   1:09.95  1:47.79  2:24.96
15    2     59 heinbuch,dave            can   33.41   1:10.04  1:46.97  2:25.29
16    6    132 lerpiniere,peter         gbr   33.60   1:10.53  1:47.65  2:25.58
17    7     28 kriechbaum,steffen       aut   32.90   1:10.21  1:47.48  2:25.73
18    2    107 kerola,tuomo             fin   33.38   1:10.35  1:47.82  2:25.87
19    7    272 shinya,tateki            jpn   34.06   1:10.99  1:48.48  2:26.16
20    1    332 gatinchi,orlando         pur   33.70   1:11.54  1:48.92  2:26.27
21    7    320 smiglak,cezary           pol   33.14   1:10.12  1:47.96  2:27.41
22    1      8 jarvie,paul              aus   33.89   1:11.37  1:50.35  2:30.15
23    1    290 lozano,gustavo           mex   33.38   1:11.61  1:51.46  2:31.89
24    8    447 divjak,zdravko           yug   36.12   1:15.57  1:54.51  2:34.07
25    8    317 abreu,emilio j.          par   35.10   1:13.70  1:54.08  2:35.22
26    8    323 carvalhovicencio,henrique por  36.24   1:17.85  1:59.89  2:41.97
27    3     40 p. ribeiro,sergio        bra                            dq
27    2    333 nazario,carlos           pur                            dq
27    2    136 naisby,paul              gbr                            dq
30    1    151 sperling,wolfram         gdr                            np
30    5    222 vermes,alban             hun                            np
```

les huit premiers se qualifient pour la finale
the first eight qualify for the final

```
piscine olympique          july 24 juil   19:30   resultats / results
natation              200 m brasse         hommes          finale
swimming              200 m breaststroke    men            final
ro/or= 2:18.29        rm/wr= 2:18.21    date/hr: 24/19:49   fin: glk

rang  coul                                  50 m    100 m    150 m     200 m
rank  lane

 1    4    143 wilkie,david          gbr   31.24   1:06.49  1:40.84  2:15.11 nrm nwr
 2    3    422 hencken,john          usa   31.32   1:06.09  1:41.50  2:17.26
 3    5    409 colella,rick          usa   32.13   1:07.44  1:42.78  2:19.20
 4    2     78 smith,graham          can   32.00   1:07.01  1:42.97  2:19.42
 5    6    424 keating,charles       usa   32.32   1:08.35  1:44.22  2:20.79
 6    7    377 iuozaytis,arvidas     urs   32.62   1:08.89  1:45.98  2:21.87
 7    1    394 pankin,nikolay        urs   32.47   1:07.83  1:44.47  2:22.21
 8    8    167 kusch,walter          ger   32.75   1:09.01  1:46.27  2:22.36
```

July 22, 1976   Montreal

4 x 100 m medley relay   final

After backstroke leg   Split time

1	USA	Naber, John	55.89
2	CAN	Pickell, Steve	57.58 n
3	GER	Steinbach, Klaus	57.82 n
4	AUS	Kerry, Mark	57.94 n
5	URS	Omelchenko, Igor	59.10 n
6	GBR	Carter, Jimmy	59.60 n
7	ITA	Bisso, Enrico	1:00.25
8	JPN	Honda, Tadashi	1:01.28

After breaststroke leg

1	USA	Hencken, John	1:02.50	1:58.39
2	CAN	Smith, Graham	1:02.59	2:00.17
3	GER	Kusch, Walter	1:03.74	2:01.56
4	GBR	Wilkie, David	1:02.81	2:02.41
5	URS	Iuozaytis, Arvidas	1:04.41	2.03.51
6	AUS	Jarvie, Paul	1:05.70	2:03.64
7	ITA	Lalle, Giorgio	1:04.33	2:04.58
8	JPN	Taguchi, Nobutaka	1:04.15	2:05.43

After butterfly leg

1	USA	Vogel, Matt	54.26	2:52.65
2	CAN	Evans, Clay	54.43	2:54.60
3	GER	Kraus, Michael	55.38	2:56.94
4	GBR	Mills, John	55.70	2:58.11
5	AUS	Rogers, Neil	55.50	2:59.14
6	URS	Seredin, Evgeniy	56.19	2:59.70
7	JPN	Hara, Hideaki	55.70	3:01.13
8	ITA	Barelli, Paolo	57.38	3:01.96

After freestyle leg

1	USA	Montgomery, Jim	49.57	3:42.22 nwr
2	CAN	Macdonald, Gary	51.34	3:45.94 cr
3	GER	Nocke, Peter	50.35	3:47.29 er
4	GBR	Brinkley, Brian	51.45	3:49.56 n
5	URS	Krylov, Andrey	50.20	3:49.90 n
6	AUS	Coughlan, Peter	52.40	3:41.54 n
7	ITA	Guarducci, Marcello	50.96	3:52.92 n
8	JPN	Yanagidate, Tsuyoshi	53.61	3:54.74 n

nwr = World record.   cr = Common 'ealth record.

er = European record.   n = national record

Amateur Swimming Association National championships

Year	Venue	100 m. breaststroke	200 m. breaststroke	200 m. medley	100 m. freestyle
'71	Worthing s/c	1:09.8 (1)	2.33.5 (1)	1:28.9 (1)	
'72	Grimsby s/c	1:10.0y (3)	2:31.6y (1)	1:28.9y (2)	
	Crystal Palace l/c	1:08.3 (2)	2:28.0 (1)	2:12.4 (2)	
'73	Coventry l/c	1:07.86 (1)	2:27.60 (1)	2:12.96 (2)	55.79 (2)
'74	Blackpool l/c	1:06.96 (1)	2:26.3 (1)	2:12.3 (1)	55.7 (2)

s/c = short course (33⅓ metres or (y) 36⅔ yards bath)

l/c = long course (50 metres pool)

These are the only championships in which Wilkie swam. After going to Miami in 1973, he was competing in the N.C.A.A. meetings at the time of the short course championships held in late March or early April. He missed the 1971 long-course A.S.A. meeting because he was on holiday in Colombo, chose not to swim in Coventry in 1975 and had retired before the 1976 meeting was held at Crystal Palace.

National Collegiate Athletic Association championships (in 25 yard pool)

Date	Venue	100 yd breaststroke	200 yd breaststroke	200 yd medley
1973	Knoxville	57.66 (4)	2:03.47 (1)	1:55.11 (13)
1974	Long Beach	56.72 (1)	2:03.40 (2)	1:52.71 (4)
1975	Cleveland	56.30 (2)	2:01.49 (disq)	1:50.67 (3)
1976	Rhode Island	56.37 (2)	*2:00.73 (1)	1:50.30 (2)

* US open record

Amateur Athletic Union championships (in 25 yard pool)

Date	Venue	100 yd breaststroke	200 yd breaststroke	200 yd medley
1973	Cincinnati	58.81 (5)	2:05.71 (3)	1:57.10 (11)
1974	Dallas	56.58 (2)	2:01.84 (2)	1:52.25 (9)
1975	Cincinnati		did not take part	
1976	Long Beach**	1:04.46 (1)	2:18.48 (1)	2:06.25 (1)e/c/b

** swum in a 50 metre pool over 100 and 200 metre distances

e/c/b = European, Commonwealth and British record

Scottish championships victories

400m freestyle:	1972	4:25.2
100m backstroke:	1973	1:02.61 sc
100m breaststroke:	1970	1:13.4
	1972	1:10.4
200m breaststroke:	1970	2:39.4
	1972	2:38.4
		(2:32.1 heat)
	1973	2:29.50
200m medley:	1972	2:15.3
400m medley:	1972	5:08.8

sc = Scottish record

Wilkie did not swim in the 1971 championships and could only take part on the first day of the 1973 meeting because he had to join the British team for the Europa Cup in East Berlin.